WHITMAN

—

THE MYSTIC POETS

WHITMAN

—

THE MYSTIC POETS

Preface by Gary David Comstock,
University Protestant Chaplain,
Wesleyan University

Walking Together, Finding the Way
SKYLIGHT PATHS® Publishing
Woodstock, Vermont

Whitman:
The Mystic Poets

2004 First Printing
© 2004 by SkyLight Paths Publishing

For information regarding permission to reprint material from this book, please write or fax your request to SkyLight Paths Publishing, Permissions Department, at the address / fax number listed below, or e-mail your request to permissions@skylightpaths.com.

Photos on pp. ii and 4 courtesy of the Bayley-Whitman Collection of Ohio Wesleyan University.

Photo on p. vi courtesy of the Library of Congress, Prints and Photographs Division LC-USZ62-89910

Library of Congress Cataloging-in-Publication Data
Whitman, Walt, 1819–1892.
[Selections. 2005]
Whitman : the mystic poets / preface by Gary David Comstock.
      p. cm.—(The mystic poets series)
Includes bibliographical references and index.
ISBN 1-59473-041-5 (hardcover)
1. Mysticism—Poetry. I. Title. II. Series.
PS3203.C66 2004
811'.3—dc22   2004014236

10 9 8 7 6 5 4 3 2 1
Manufactured in Canada
Jacket Design: Bridgett Taylor and Jenny Buono

SkyLight Paths Publishing is creating a place where people of different spiritual traditions come together for challenge and inspiration, a place where we can help each other understand the mystery that lies at the heart of our existence.

SkyLight Paths sees both believers and seekers as a community that increasingly transcends traditional boundaries of religion and denomination—people wanting to learn from each other, *walking together, finding the way.*

SkyLight Paths, "Walking Together, Finding the Way" and colophon are trademarks of LongHill Partners, Inc., registered in the U.S. Patent and Trademark Office.

Walking Together, Finding the Way
Published by SkyLight Paths Publishing
A Division of LongHill Partners, Inc.
Sunset Farm Offices, Route 4, P.O. Box 237
Woodstock, VT 05091
Tel: (802) 457-4000   Fax: (802) 457-4004
www.skylightpaths.com

Contents

Preface

Rev. Dr. Gary David Comstock

Imagining how my life would have unfolded without the words and ideas of Walt Whitman is very difficult. I cannot say for sure that I would have realized that I could and should "celebrate myself," if Whitman's poetry had not found me and disrupted my efforts to be normal and to fit in at any expense. Throughout the ages, prophets have emerged on the fringes of tribes and societies to remind and encourage us to value and exercise our personal interests and feelings against the weight of restrictive convention. Absent political authority or social favor, they manage to get their message to us through the backdoor, giving us permission to become ourselves instead of becoming what others want us to be.

The ancient Hebrew prophet Isaiah urged his people to avoid the elaborate but empty religious rituals of his day and to attend to their personal feelings— "to bind up the broken hearted" and to do so with "the mantle of praise instead of a faint spirit." In his 1838 address to graduating clergy from Harvard, Ralph Waldo Emerson insisted that "intuition," received and exchanged firsthand among people, stands over whatever abstract truth may be issued from the academy or organized religion. And today, the lesbian Chicana activist Gloria Anzaldúa, in *This Bridge Called My Back,* sounds a similar note when she says, "I'm trying to create a religion not out there somewhere, but in my gut," and inspires us to do the same.

Whitman, too, warns against trusting and giving oneself over to the guardians and promoters of established truth and knowledge. As he writes in his "Open Letter to Ralph Waldo Emerson," "The priests are continually telling what they know well enough is not so, and keeping back what they know is so." His voice, so fresh and challenging in the nineteenth century, remains so today because he refuses to replace the established authority with yet another that would in turn have to be abided or knocked over. Whitman does not present himself or another as a model to be imitated and admired. Instead, he invites us in *Leaves of Grass* to "stand by my side and look in the mirror with me."

Whitman's collected poems and prose are not an object or icon to be gazed upon or revered but a transparency we can look through to see ourselves with greater clarity, excitement, and meaning. They wake us up to our potential, to learning about and from ourselves. In "Who Learns My Lesson Complete?" he describes the awesome beauty of all creation in gracious and grateful detail, and then includes and honors us by reaching not just out to but into us: "Come I should like to hear you tell me what there is in yourself that is not just as wonderful." To experience his writing is to experience ourselves more deeply, to recognize and embrace what he calls in "Burial Poem" the "something long preparing and formless" that has "arrived and formed" in each of us.

I am fond of Whitman's seemingly endless lists of all types of people, in which the rhythm builds and excites, criticizing implicitly those who exclude or despise some people, and embodying the optimism of his not wanting "a single person slighted," as he says in "I Sound Triumphal Drums for the Dead." At times I feel slightly bored with these lists, but this feeling jogs me into remembering that they are not a complete or final answer, not a perfect model of inclusivity. They are a process awaiting my participation, an invitation to contribute my own entries of what Whitman has left out. His writing discourages a passive, obedient reading and instead calls us to celebrate that within us and those among us in need of being celebrated.

Who Is Walt Whitman?

Walt Whitman (1819–1892) is widely considered the most important poet in the history of American literature. He took part in that great mid-nineteenth-century renaissance that included the publication of Herman Melville's novel *Moby-Dick*, Henry David Thoreau's travel journal *A Week on the Concord and Merrimac Rivers* and his naturalistic manifesto *Walden*, the writings and lectures of Margaret Fuller and Nathaniel Hawthorne, and the spiritual leadership of Ralph Waldo Emerson, "father" to them all.

Although Whitman's stature as an innovator of ideas and spirit is great, his reputation was earned industriously during his lifetime. Whitman self-published the first edition of his now-famous book *Leaves of Grass* in 1855. He relentlessly self-promoted those initial 795 copies, writing anonymous reviews, sending promotional packets to members of the media, and galvanizing a movement with himself as its primary instigator and leader. Anyone who is lucky enough to find one of those first-edition copies tucked away in an attic can sell it for its fair market value of about $60,000.

Both his personality and his work inspired strong feelings in others. There are very few people who knew Whitman during his lifetime who did not have a strongly held opinion about him. One New York City journalist and anthologist of poetry, Rufus Griswold (a contemporary of Whitman's), wrote that *Leaves of Grass*—which comprised only twelve untitled poems and one very long preface in that first edition—was "a mass of stupid filth." Griswold's review was typical of others at the time that seemed to view the poetry as a personal attack on their way of life. Whitman's poetry was wrapped up in his public persona, and his public persona displayed what he felt America needed at that time and place. But Griswold continued disapprovingly, "There was a time when licentiousness laughed at reproval; now it writes essays and delivers lectures."

Whitman was nothing if not self-conscious, and the confessional mode of his poetry was shocking to many of his contemporaries. His use of the personal pronoun "I" was revolutionary, but in poetry today it is commonplace. Whitman always wrote in his own voice, and his poems clearly expressed his view of the world as it was and as it should be.

He wrote anonymous reviews of his own poems, particularly after that first private printing of *Leaves of Grass*. When acting as his own publicist, he was known to enclose copies of the worst reviews he had received in the press when sending new review copies to the media. He was witty and hilarious, and he enjoyed the energy of the give and take of his own ideas.

Below are some typical paragraphs from a review of the first edition of *Leaves of Grass,* which was written anonymously by Whitman himself for the *United States Review,* published in September 1855. The beginnings of the first and third paragraphs make reference to the frontispiece photo of Whitman that he delighted in including in his book. (The same photo appears on p. ii of this SkyLight Paths volume.) This review demonstrates how the movement that Whitman desired to create and sustain was not only about ideas but about appearances too. In the fourth paragraph, Whitman announces the dramatically new style of his own poetry:

An American bard at last! One of the roughs, large, proud, affectionate, eating, drinking, and breeding, his costume manly and free, his face sunburnt and bearded, his posture strong and erect, his voice bringing hope and prophecy to the generous races of young and old. We shall cease shamming and be what we really are. We shall start an athletic and defiant literature. We realize now how it is, and what was most lacking. The interior American republic shall also be declared free and independent.

For all our intellectual people, followed by their books, poems, novels, essays, editorials, lectures, tuitions, and criticism, dress by London and Paris modes, receive what is received there, obey the authorities, settle disputes by the old tests, keep out of rain and sun, retreat to the shelter of houses and schools, trim their hair, shave, touch not the earth barefoot, and enter not the sea except in a complete bathing-dress. One sees unmistakably genteel persons, travelled, college-learned, used to be served by servants, conversing without heat or vulgarity, supported on chairs, or walking through handsomely-carpeted parlors, or along shelves bearing well-bound volumes, and walls adorned with curtained and collared portraits, and china things, and nick-nacks. But where in American literature is the first show of America? Where are the gristle and beards, and broad breasts, and space and ruggedness and nonchalance that the souls of the people love? Where is the tremendous outdoors of these States? Where is the majesty of the federal mother, seated with more than antique grace, calm, just, indulgent to her brood of children, calling them around her regarding the little and the large and the younger and the older with perfect impartiality? Where is the vehement growth of our cities? Where is the spirit of the strong rich life of the American mechanic, farmer, sailor, hunter, and miner? Where is the huge composite of all other nations, cast in a fresher and brawnier matrix, passing adolescence, and needed this day, live and arrogant, to lead the marches of the world?

Self-reliant, with haughty eyes, assuming to himself all the attributes of his country, steps Walt Whitman into literature, talking like a man unaware that there was ever hitherto such a production as a book, or such a being as a writer. Every move of him has the free play of the muscle of one who never knew what it was to feel that he stood in the presence of a superior. Every word that falls from his mouth shows silent disdain and defiance of the old theories and forms. Every phrase announces new laws; not once do his lips unclose except in conformity with them. With light and rapid touch he first indicates in prose the principles of the foundation of a race of poets so deeply to spring from the American people, and become ingrained through them, that their Presidents shall not be the common referees so much as that great race of poets shall. He proceeds himself to exemplify this new school, and set models for their expression and range of subjects. He makes audacious and native use of his own body and soul. He must re-create poetry with the elements always at hand. He must imbue it with himself as he is, disorderly, fleshy, and sensual, a lover of things, yet a lover of men and women above the whole of the other objects of the universe....

The style of these poems, therefore, is simply their own style, new-born and red. Nature may have given the hint to the author of the *Leaves of Grass*, but there exists no book or fragment of a book, which can have given the hint to them. All beauty, he says, comes from beautiful blood and a beautiful brain. His rhythm and uniformity he will conceal in the roots of his verses, not to be seen of themselves, but to break forth loosely as lilies on a bush, and take shapes compact as the shapes of melons, or chestnuts, or pears.

The poems of the *Leaves of Grass* are twelve in number. Walt Whitman at first proceeds to put his own body and soul into the new versification:

> I celebrate myself,
> And what I assume you shall assume,
> For every atom belonging to me, as good belongs to you.

He leaves houses and their shuttered rooms, for the open air. He drops disguise and ceremony, and walks forth with the confidence and gayety of a child. For the old decorums of writing he substitutes new decorums. The first glance out of his eyes electrifies him with love and delight. He will have the earth receive and return his affection; he will stay with it as the bride-groom stays with the bride. The cool-breathed ground, the slumbering and liquid trees, the just-gone sunset, the vitreous pour of the full moon, the tender and growing night, he salutes and touches, and they touch him. The sea supports him, and hurries him off with its powerful and crooked fingers. Dash me with amorous wet! then he says, I can repay you.

By this writer the rules of polite circles are dismissed with scorn. Your stale modesties, he says, are filthy to such a man as I.

> I believe in the flesh and the appetites,
> Seeing, hearing, and feeling are miracles, and each part and tag of me is a miracle.

> I do not press my finger across my mouth,
> I keep as delicate around the bowels as around
> > the head and heart.

No sniveller, or tea-drinking poet, no puny clawback or prude, is Walt Whitman. He will bring poems fit to fill the days and nights—fit for men and women with the attributes of throbbing blood and flesh. The body, he teaches, is beautiful. Sex is also beautiful. Are you to be put down, he seems to ask, to that shallow level of literature and conversation that stops a man's recognizing the delicious pleasure of his sex, or a woman hers? Nature he proclaims inherently pure. Sex will not be put aside; it is a great ordination of the universe. He works the muscle of the male and the teeming fibre of the female throughout his writings, as wholesome realities, impure only by deliberate intention and effort. To men and women he says: You can have healthy and powerful breeds of children on no less terms than these of mine. Follow me and there shall be taller and nobler crops of humanity on the earth.

Those last paragraphs of Whitman's self-review provide an indication of what most alarmed his contemporaries: his celebration of the sensuous. Puritan feeling was all too prominent in Whitman's day to allow for any celebration of flesh, beauty, pleasure, or even sex.

Toward the conclusion of Whitman's "review" are these additional paragraphs declaring himself the ideal new physical and intellectual type, self-made for a new era emerging in America:

> Who then is that insolent unknown? Who is it, praising himself as if others were not fit to do it, and coming rough and unbidden among writers to unsettle what was settled, and to revolutionize, in fact, our modern civilization? Walt Whitman was born on Long-Island, on the hills about thirty miles from the greatest American city, on the last day of May, 1819, and has grown up in Brooklyn and New York to be thirty-six years old, to enjoy perfect health, and to understand his country and its spirit.
>
> Interrogations more than this, and that will not be put off unanswered, spring continually through the perusal of these Leaves of Grass: If there were to be selected, out of the incalculable volumes of printed matter in existence, any single work to stand for America and her times, should this be the work?
>
> Must not the true American poet indeed absorb all others, and present a new and far more ample and vigorous type?
>
> Has not the time arrived for a school of live writing and tuition consistent with the principles of these poems? consistent with the free spirit of this age, and with the American truths of politics? consistent with geology, and astronomy, and all science and human physiology? consistent with the sublimity of immortality and the directness of common-sense?

If in this poem the United States have found their poetic voice, and taken measure and form, is it any more than a beginning? Walt Whitman himself disclaims singularity in his work, and announces the coming after him of great successions of poets, and that he but lifts his finger to give the signal.

Was he not needed? Has not literature been bred in and in long enough? Has it not become unbearably artificial?

Shall a man of faith and practice in the simplicity of real things be called eccentric, while the disciple of the fictitious school writes without question?

Shall it still be the amazement of the light and dark that freshness of expression is the rarest quality of all?

You have come in good time, Walt Whitman! In opinions, in manners, in costumes, in books, in the aims and occupancy of life, in associates, in poems, conformity to all unnatural and tainted customs passes without remark, while perfect naturalness, health, faith, self-reliance, and all primal expressions of the manliest love and friendship, subject one to the stare and controversy of the world.

Whitman shocked and challenged his contemporaries to see beyond the norms and expectations of society. He would lead them to see that the spiritual is not contained in decorum but in spirit. "I cock my hat as I please indoors or out. / Shall I pray? Shall I venerate and be ceremonious?" (from "Do You Guess I Have Some Intricate Purpose?" p. 69).

A Short Introduction to Whitman's Mysticism

Like Religion, Love, Nature, while those terms are indispensable, and we all give a sufficiently accurate meaning to them, in my opinion no definition that has ever been made sufficiently encloses the name Poetry.

—WALT WHITMAN,
"A BACKWARD GLANCE O'ER TRAVEL'D ROADS" (1888)

Whitman sought to tear down the belief that the spiritual resides only in the religious. In the whole universe, he believed, there is nothing more divine than humankind, and all of the universe is divine as well. These ideas were beginning to emerge from the spiritual traditions of the East during Whitman's lifetime, and he embraced them with his whole heart and through the vigor of his poems.

Whitman also taught that the soul is no greater than the body and God is no greater than one's individual self. One of his first poems in *Leaves of Grass*—which was revised into a poem titled "A Song for Occupations" in later editions—explains:

> I do not affirm that what you see beyond is
>   futile . . . . I do not advise you to stop,
> I do not say leadings you thought great are not
>   great,

But I say that none lead to greater or sadder or
    happier than those lead to.
…
When the psalm sings instead of the singer,
When the script preaches instead of the
    preacher,
…
When the sacred vessels or the bits of the
    eucharist, or the lath and plast, procreate as
    effectually as the young silversmiths or bak-
    ers, or the masons in their overalls,

One of his first biographers, Richard Maurice Bucke, published this explanation in 1883 from a letter written by Helen Price, a close friend of the poet: "If I were asked what I considered Walt Whitman's leading characteristic, I should say—and it is an opinion formed upon an acquaintance of over twenty years—his religious sentiment or feeling…. His is not that religion, or show of it, that is comprised in dogmas, churches, creeds, etc. These are of little or no consequence to him, but it is that habitual state of feeling in which the person regards everything in God's universe with wonder, reverence, perfect acceptance, and love."

Whitman's prevailing optimism and joy are all the more interesting because they were nurtured by real sadness. He knew severe difficulty and loss. The second of nine children, four of whom were physically disabled, Whitman grew up in a poor home and left school as a young boy in order to work to help support his family. He learned the trade of a newspaperman, which in nineteenth-century New York City was just about the best job possible for feeding a voracious appetite for meeting people.

Later in life, after he had already begun to achieve fame for his writing and lecturing, he served as a volunteer nurse for the Union Army during the Civil War. Whitman witnessed many terrible things, such as amputations and other grisly sights, which would find their way into the poetry as he praised the determination of the American spirit. There is nothing saccharine in Whitman's spirituality. He explains the origin of the title of his book *Leaves of Grass* when he writes: "I believe a leaf of grass is no less than the journeywork of the stars."

He was an intellectual as well, although one would never have known it by looking at him or listening to him talk. Though a son of uneducated parents, Whitman still managed to read widely but without becoming bookish. Reading was self-discovery for Whitman, and self-discovery was an ongoing mystical experience of the world. In this autobiographical passage he describes the reading of his late teenage years:

> Later, at intervals, summers and falls, I used to go off, sometimes for a week at a stretch, down in the country, or to Long Island's seashores—there, in the presence of outdoor influences, I went over thoroughly the Old and New Testaments, and absorb'd (probably to better advantage for me than in any

library or indoor room—it makes such difference where you read,) Shakspere, Ossian, the best translated versions I could get of Homer, Eschylus, Sophocles, the old German Nibelungen, the ancient Hindoo poems, and one or two other masterpieces, Dante's among them. As it happen'd, I read the latter mostly in an old wood. The Iliad … I read first thoroughly on the peninsula of Orient, northeast end of Long Island, in a shelter'd hollow of rocks and sand, with the sea on each side. (I have wonder'd since why I was not overwhelm'd by those mighty masters. Likely because I read them, as described, in the full presence of Nature, under the sun, with the far-spreading landscape and vistas, or the sea rolling in.)[1]

Readers unfamiliar with Whitman often make the mistake of thinking that he is a nature poet. Quite the contrary. While his contemporary Henry David Thoreau was spending all day walking in the woods around Concord, Massachusetts, Whitman was walking the rough streets of New York City. When George Ripley and others of his contemporaries were founding rural, utopian communities such as Brook Farm outside Boston in order to focus on "plain living and high thinking," Whitman was following a different course.

His spirituality was aimed at uniting himself as much as possible, in spirit and body, with his neighbors. And he sang his neighbors' praises throughout his poems, for seemingly the simplest things. For example, in one of the first *Leaves of Grass* poems, quoted in full on page 54, Whitman writes this memorable line about walking outdoors: "The press of my foot to the earth springs a hundred affections," only to follow it with: "I am enamoured of growing outdoors, / Of men that live among cattle or taste of the ocean or woods, / Of the builders and steerers of ships, of the wielders of axes and mauls, of the drivers of horses, / I can eat and sleep with them week in and week out."

Whitman was the first major poet to make humanity his subject. He was also the first poet in America, and perhaps the most eloquent poet to write in English, who championed the body as a subject worth praise. Love, sex, work, courage, hope, and strength are all subjects of the poems in *Leaves of Grass,* and each is put into the context of the inestimable value of the human body. It is widely documented that Whitman was homosexual in orientation, but that is far from his only concern in the poems praising the human being and its abilities, strengths, and glories. In fact, the "Calamus" section of *Leaves of Grass*—which caused so much controversy in Whitman's day—was not introduced until the book's third edition (1860). That year, Whitman took a stroll with Ralph Waldo Emerson, his spiritual and intellectual hero, who advised him to delete these poems before going to press, but Whitman refused.

Whitman intended *Leaves of Grass* to reinvigorate a spiritual and intellectual movement that had fallen dormant compared with its influence one to two decades earlier: Transcendentalism. Ralph Waldo Emerson,

Henry David Thoreau, and Bronson Alcott were among Whitman's first literary admirers, and each became his good friend. But Whitman's approach to the tenets of Transcendentalism was different from that of most of his contemporaries. Thoreau experimented on Walden Pond, and others sought utopia at Brook Farm, in the belief that the material aspects of society—our need to make an income, pay taxes to support our community, and so on—are secondary in importance to the spiritual conditions of life. Whitman believed the same, but he did not share the idea that a perfect society would come from disengagement with the world around him, and he celebrated the baser aspects of economy, work, soil, even violence, that he believed are also a part of the overall goodness of our world.

A few excerpts from Emerson's foundational "Divinity School Address," given at Harvard in 1838, which became the "scripture" of the Transcendentalist movement, help to paint the picture of Whitman's spiritual worldview.

> In this refulgent summer, it has been a luxury to draw the breath of life. The grass grows, the buds burst, the meadow is spotted with fire and gold in the tint of flowers. The air is full of birds, and sweet with the breath of the pine, the balm-of-Gilead, and the new hay. Night brings no gloom to the heart with its welcome shade. Through the transparent darkness the stars pour their almost spiritual rays. Man under them seems a young child, and his huge

globe a toy. The cool night bathes the world as with a river, and prepares his eyes again for the crimson dawn. The mystery of nature was never displayed more happily. The corn and the wine have been freely dealt to all creatures, and the never-broken silence with which the old bounty goes forward, has not yielded yet one word of explanation. One is constrained to respect the perfection of this world, in which our senses converse. How wide; how rich; what invitation from every property it gives to every faculty of man! In its fruitful soils; in its navigable sea; in its mountains of metal and stone; in its forests of all woods; in its animals; in its chemical ingredients; in the powers and path of light, heat, attraction, and life, it is well worth the pith and heart of great men to subdue and enjoy it. The planters, the mechanics, the inventors, the astronomers, the builders of cities, and the captains, history delights to honor.

But when the mind opens, and reveals the laws which traverse the universe, and make things what they are, then shrinks the great world at once into a mere illustration and fable of this mind. What am I? and What is? asks the human spirit with a curiosity new-kindled, but never to be quenched. Behold these outrunning laws, which our imperfect apprehension can see tend this way and that, but not come full circle. Behold these infinite relations, so like, so unlike; many, yet one. I would study, I would know,

I would admire forever. These works of thought have been the entertainments of the human spirit in all ages....

This sentiment is divine and deifying. It is the beatitude of man. It makes him illimitable. Through it, the soul first knows itself. It corrects the capital mistake of the infant man, who seeks to be great by following the great, and hopes to derive advantages from another,—by showing the fountain of all good to be in himself, and that he, equally with every man, is an inlet into the deeps of Reason. When he says, "I ought;" when love warms him; when he chooses, warned from on high, the good and great deed; then, deep melodies wander through his soul from Supreme Wisdom. Then he can worship, and be enlarged by his worship; for he can never go behind this sentiment. In the sublimest flights of the soul, rectitude is never surmounted, love is never outgrown....

Meantime, whilst the doors of the temple stand open, night and day, before every man, and the oracles of this truth cease never, it is guarded by one stern condition; this, namely; it is an intuition. It cannot be received at second hand. Truly speaking, it is not instruction, but provocation, that I can receive from another soul. What he announces, I must find true in me, or wholly reject; and on his word, or as his second, be he who he may, I can accept nothing. On the contrary, the absence of this primary faith is the presence of degradation. As is the flood so is the ebb. Let this faith depart, and the very words it spake, and the things it made, become false and hurtful. Then falls the church, the state, art, letters, life. The doctrine of the divine nature being forgotten, a sickness infects and dwarfs the constitution. Once man was all; now he is an appendage, a nuisance. And because the indwelling Supreme Spirit cannot wholly be got rid of, the doctrine of it suffers this perversion, that the divine nature is attributed to one or two persons, and denied to all the rest, and denied with fury. The doctrine of inspiration is lost; the base doctrine of the majority of voices, usurps the place of the doctrine of the soul. Miracles, prophecy, poetry; the ideal life, the holy life, exist as ancient history merely; they are not in the belief, nor in the aspiration of society; but, when suggested, seem ridiculous. Life is comic or pitiful, as soon as the high ends of being fade out of sight, and man becomes near-sighted, and can only attend to what addresses the senses.

These general views, which, whilst they are general, none will contest, find abundant illustration in the history of religion, and especially in the history of the Christian church. In that, all of us have had our birth and nurture. The truth contained in that, you, my young friends, are now setting forth to teach....

Jesus Christ belonged to the true race of prophets. He saw with open eye the mystery of the soul. Drawn by its severe harmony, ravished with its beauty, he lived in it, and had his being there. Alone in all history, he estimated the greatness of man. One man was true to what is in you and me. He saw that God incarnates himself in man, and evermore goes forth anew to take possession of his world. He said, in this jubilee of sublime emotion, "I am divine. Through me, God acts; through me, speaks. Would you see God, see me; or, see thee, when thou also thinkest as I now think." But what a distortion did his doctrine and memory suffer in the same, in the next, and the following ages! There is no doctrine of the Reason which will bear to be taught by the Understanding. The understanding caught this high chant from the poet's lips, and said, in the next age, "This was Jehovah come down out of heaven. I will kill you, if you say he was a man." The idioms of his language, and the figures of his rhetoric, have usurped the place of his truth; and churches are not built on his principles, but on his tropes. Christianity became a Mythus, as the poetic teaching of Greece and of Egypt, before. He spoke of miracles; for he felt that man's life was a miracle, and all that man doth, and he knew that this daily miracle shines, as the character ascends. But the word Miracle, as pronounced by Christian churches, gives a false impression; it is Monster. It is not one with the blowing clover and the falling rain.

He felt respect for Moses and the prophets; but no unfit tenderness at postponing their initial revelations, to the hour and the man that now is; to the eternal revelation in the heart. Thus was he a true man. Having seen that the law in us is commanding, he would not suffer it to be commanded. Boldly, with hand, and heart, and life, he declared it was God. Thus is he, as I think, the only soul in history who has appreciated the worth of a man....

Let me admonish you, first of all, to go alone; to refuse the good models, even those which are sacred in the imagination of men, and dare to love God without mediator or veil. Friends enough you shall find who will hold up to your emulation Wesleys and Oberlins, Saints and Prophets. Thank God for these good men, but say, "I also am a man." Imitation cannot go above its model. The imitator dooms himself to hopeless mediocrity. The inventor did it, because it was natural to him, and so in him it has a charm. In the imitator, something else is natural, and he bereaves himself of his own beauty, to come short of another man's.

Yourself a newborn bard of the Holy Ghost,—cast behind you all conformity, and acquaint men at first hand with Deity. Look to it first and only, that fashion, custom, authority, pleasure, and money, are nothing to you,—are not bandages over your eyes, that you cannot see,—but live with the privilege of the immeasurable mind. Not too anxious to visit periodically all families and each family in your parish connection,—when you meet one of these men or women, be to them a divine man; be to them thought and virtue; let their timid aspirations find in you a friend; let their trampled instincts be genially tempted out in your atmosphere; let their doubts know that you have doubted, and their wonder feel that you have wondered. By trusting your own heart, you shall gain more confidence in other men. For all our penny-wisdom, for all our soul-destroying slavery to habit, it is not to be doubted, that all men have sublime thoughts; that all men value the few real hours of life; they love to be heard; they love to be caught up into the vision of principles. We mark with light in the memory the few interviews we have had, in the dreary years of routine and of sin, with souls that made our souls wiser; that spoke what we thought; that told us what we knew; that gave us leave to be what we only were. Discharge to men the priestly office, and, present or absent, you shall be followed with their love as by an angel....

I look for the hour when that supreme Beauty, which ravished the souls of those eastern men, and chiefly of those Hebrews, and through their lips spoke oracles to all time, shall speak in the West also. The Hebrew and Greek Scriptures contain immortal sentences, that have been bread of life to millions. But they have no epical integrity; are fragmentary; are not shown in their order to the intellect. I look for the new Teacher, that shall follow so far those shining laws, that he shall see them come full circle; shall see their rounding complete grace; shall see the world to be the mirror of the soul; shall see the identity of the law of gravitation with purity of heart; and shall show that the Ought, that Duty, is one thing with Science, with Beauty, and with Joy.

Emerson's lines came to describe Walt Whitman, which for Whitman was no accident. "Yourself a newborn bard of the Holy Ghost,—cast behind you all conformity, and acquaint men at first hand with Deity." Whitman made sure of it, embodying Emerson's dramatic new vision for a spirituality that depends not on houses of worship but rather on the creative emergence of the human being in all its earthiness, personality, and spirit.

Describing the newness of Whitman's ideas and perspective, Harold Bloom writes:

He can be regarded as the poet proper of what I think may yet be called the American religion, which is post-Christian (though few will admit this). Pentecostalists, Mormons, and Emersonians (among others) have little or no continuity with European Protestantisms. Their ancestry is elsewhere, with heretical strains of Enthusiasm, Hermeticism, and Neo-Platonism. Whitman, though inspired by Emerson, was eclectic and more of an Epicurean materialist than a Transcendental idealist.[2]

Finally, and perhaps most important at this particular time in the history of America, Whitman's poems are full of a spirituality of patriotism. He keenly felt the special place of America in the world, and he expressed this throughout his verse. His patriotism is a democracy for all people, and his love of country is as wide and inclusive as can be. He wrote as one who had seen the horrors of war firsthand and understood how all living things fit together.

> It is for the endless races of working people and farmers and seamen.
>
> This is the trill of a thousand clear cornets and scream of the octave flute and strike of triangles.
>
> I play not a march for victors only…. I play great marches for conquered and slain persons.
>
> Have you heard that it was good to gain the day?
>
> I also say it is good to fall … battles are lost in the same spirit in which they are won.

(from "I Am of Old and Young, of the Foolish as Much as the Wise," p. 60)

Poems from *Leaves of Grass* —the first edition (1855)

Note to readers: Each of the twelve long, multistanza poems in the first edition of *Leaves of Grass* was entitled "Leaves of Grass." Lines did not rhyme, and there was no apparent meter, which obviously confused Whitman's first readers but seems perfectly natural to us today.

Each of the poems that follow represents a group of stanzas from the original edition. For the sake of clarity and easy reference, each group of stanzas is given the simple title of its first line. These verses present Whitman's ideas and spirit in their first, rough-cut form.

In later editions of *Leaves of Grass*, all the stanzas that follow were part of one long poem that came to be called "Song of Myself."

I Celebrate Myself

I celebrate myself,
And what I assume you shall assume,
For every atom belonging to me as good belongs
    to you.

I loafe and invite my soul,
I lean and loafe at my ease . . . . observing a spear
    of summer grass.

Houses and rooms are full of perfumes . . . . the
    shelves are crowded with perfumes,
I breathe the fragrance myself, and know it and
    like it,
The distillation would intoxicate me also, but I
    shall not let it.

The atmosphere is not a perfume . . . . it has no
    taste of the distillation . . . . it is odorless,
It is for my mouth forever . . . . I am in love with it,
I will go to the bank by the wood and become
    undisguised and naked,
I am mad for it to be in contact with me.

The smoke of my own breath,
Echos, ripples, and buzzed whispers . . . . loveroot,
    silkthread, crotch and vine,

My respiration and inspiration . . . . the beating of
    my heart . . . . the passing of blood and air
    through my lungs,
The sniff of green leaves and dry leaves, and of the
    shore and darkcolored sea-rocks, and of hay in
    the barn,
The sound of the belched words of my voice . . . .
    words loosed to the eddies of the wind,
A few light kisses . . . . a few embraces . . . . a
    reaching around of arms,
The play of shine and shade on the trees as the
    supple boughs wag,
The delight alone or in the rush of the streets, or
    along the fields and hillsides,
The feeling of health . . . . the full-noon trill . . . .
    the song of me rising from bed and meeting the
    sun.

Have You Reckoned a Thousand Acres Much?

Have you reckoned a thousand acres much? Have
    you reckoned the earth much?
Have you practiced so long to learn to read?
Have you felt so proud to get at the meaning of
    poems?

Stop this day and night with me and you shall
    possess the origin of all poems,
You shall possess the good of the earth and
    sun . . . . there are millions of suns left,
You shall no longer take things at second or third
    hand . . . . nor look through the eyes of the
    dead . . . . nor feed on the spectres in books,
You shall not look through my eyes either, nor
    take things from me,
You shall listen to all sides and filter them from
    yourself.

I have heard what the talkers were talking . . . .
    the talk of the beginning and the end,
But I do not talk of the beginning or the end.

There was never any more inception than there is
    now,
Nor any more youth or age than there is now;
And will never be any more perfection than there
    is now,

Nor any more heaven or hell than there is now.

Urge and urge and urge,
Always the procreant urge of the world.

Out of the dimness opposite equals advance . . . .
    Always substance and increase,
Always a knit of identity . . . . always distinction . . . .
    always a breed of life.

To elaborate is no avail . . . . Learned and
    unlearned feel that it is so.

Sure as the most certain sure . . . . plumb in the
    uprights, well entretied, braced in the beams,
Stout as a horse, affectionate, haughty, electrical,
I and this mystery here we stand.

Clear and sweet is my soul . . . . and clear and
    sweet is all that is not my soul.

Lack one lacks both . . . . and the unseen is proved
    by the seen,
Till that becomes unseen and receives proof in its
    turn.

Showing the best and dividing it from the worst,
    age vexes age,
Knowing the perfect fitness and equanimity of
    things, while they discuss I am silent, and go
    bathe and admire myself.

Welcome is every organ and attribute of me, and of
    any man hearty and clean,
Not an inch nor a particle of an inch is vile, and
    none shall be less familiar than the rest.

I Am Satisfied .... I See,
Dance, Laugh, Sing

I am satisfied .... I see, dance, laugh, sing;
As God comes a loving bedfellow and sleeps at my
    side all night and close on the peep of the day,
And leaves for me baskets covered with white
    towels bulging the house with their plenty,
Shall I postpone my acceptation and realization
    and scream at my eyes,
That they turn from gazing after and down the
    road,
And forthwith cipher and show me to a cent,
Exactly the contents of one, and exactly the
    contents of two, and which is ahead?

Trippers and askers surround me,
People I meet ..... the effect upon me of my early
    life .... of the ward and city I live in .... of
    the nation,
The latest news .... discoveries, inventions,
    societies .... authors old and new,
My dinner, dress, associates, looks, business,
    compliments, dues,
The real or fancied indifference of some man or
    woman I love,
The sickness of one of my folks—or of myself ....
    or ill-doing .... or loss or lack of money ....
    or depressions or exaltations,

They come to me days and nights and go from me
	again,
But they are not the Me myself.

Apart from the pulling and hauling stands what I
	am,
Stands amused, complacent, compassionating, idle,
	unitary,
Looks down, is erect, bends an arm on an
	impalpable certain rest,
Looks with its sidecurved head curious what will
	come next,
Both in and out of the game, and watching and
	wondering at it.

Backward I see in my own days where I sweated
	through fog with linguists and contenders,
I have no mockings or arguments . . . . I witness
	and wait.

I Believe in You My Soul

I believe in you my soul . . . . the other I am must
   not abase itself to you,
And you must not be abased to the other.

Loafe with me on the grass . . . . loose the stop
   from your throat,
Not words, not music or rhyme I want . . . . not
   custom or lecture, not even the best,
Only the lull I like, the hum of your valved voice.

I mind how we lay in June, such a transparent
   summer morning;
You settled your head athwart my hips and gently
   turned over upon me,
And parted the shirt from my bosom-bone, and
   plunged your tongue to my barestript heart,
And reached till you felt my beard, and reached till
   you held my feet.

Swiftly arose and spread around me the peace and
   joy and knowledge that pass all the art and
   argument of the earth;
And I know that the hand of God is the elderhand
   of my own,
And I know that the spirit of God is the eldest
   brother of my own,

And that all the men ever born are also my
  brothers . . . . and the women my sisters and
  lovers,
And that a kelson of the creation is love;
And limitless are leaves stiff or drooping in the
  fields,
And brown ants in the little wells beneath them,
And mossy scabs of the wormfence, and heaped
  stones, and elder and mullen and pokeweed.

A Child Said, What Is the Grass?
Fetching It to Me with Full Hands

A child said, What is the grass? fetching it to me
    with full hands;
How could I answer the child? . . . . I do not know
    what it is any more than he.

I guess it must be the flag of my disposition, out of
    hopeful green stuff woven.

Or I guess it is the handkerchief of the Lord,
A scented gift and remembrancer designedly
    dropped,
Bearing the owner's name someway in the corners,
    that we may see and remark, and say Whose?

Or I guess the grass is itself a child . . . . the
    produced babe of the vegetation.

Or I guess it is a uniform hieroglyphic,
And it means, Sprouting alike in broad zones and
    narrow zones,
Growing among black folks as among white,
Kanuck, Tuckahoe, Congressman, Cuff, I give
    them the same, I receive them the same.

And now it seems to me the beautiful uncut hair of
    graves.

Tenderly will I use you curling grass,
It may be you transpire from the breasts of young
men,
It may be if I had known them I would have loved
them;
It may be you are from old people and from
women, and from offspring taken soon out of
their mothers' laps,
And here you are the mothers' laps.

This grass is very dark to be from the white heads
of old mothers,
Darker than the colorless beards of old men,
Dark to come from under the faint red roofs of
mouths.

O I perceive after all so many uttering tongues!
And I perceive they do not come from the roofs of
mouths for nothing.

I Wish I Could Translate the Hints

I wish I could translate the hints about the dead
    young men and women,
And the hints about old men and mothers, and the
    offspring taken soon out of their laps.

What do you think has become of the young and
    old men?
And what do you think has become of the women
    and children?

They are alive and well somewhere;
The smallest sprout shows there is really no death,
And if ever there was it led forward life, and does
    not wait at the end to arrest it,
And ceased the moment life appeared.

All goes onward and outward . . . . and nothing
    collapses,
And to die is different from what any one
    supposed, and luckier.

Has any one supposed it lucky to be born?
I hasten to inform him or her it is just as lucky to
    die, and I know it.

I pass death with the dying, and birth with the
    new-washed babe . . . . and am not contained
    between my hat and boots,
And peruse manifold objects, no two alike, and
    every one good,
The earth good, and the stars good, and their
    adjuncts all good.

I am not an earth nor an adjunct of an earth,
I am the mate and companion of people, all just as
    immortal and fathomless as myself;
They do not know how immortal, but I know.

Every kind for itself and its own . . . . for me mine
    male and female,
For me all that have been boys and that love
    women,
For me the man that is proud and feels how it
    stings to be slighted,
For me the sweetheart and the old maid . . . . for
    me mothers and the mothers of mothers,
For me lips that have smiled, eyes that have shed
    tears,
For me children and the begetters of children.

Who need be afraid of the merge?
Undrape . . . . you are not guilty to me, nor stale
    nor discarded,
I see through the broadcloth and gingham whether
    or no,
And am around, tenacious, acquisitive, tireless . . . .
    and can never be shaken away.

The little one sleeps in its cradle,
I lift the gauze and look a long time, and silently
    brush away flies with my hand.

The youngster and the redfaced girl turn aside up
    the bushy hill,
I peeringly view them from the top.

The suicide sprawls on the bloody floor of the
    bedroom.
It is so . . . . I witnessed the corpse . . . . there the
    pistol had fallen.

The Blab of the Pave

The blab of the pave . . . . the tires of carts and sluff
    of bootsoles and talk of the promenaders,
The heavy omnibus, the driver with his
    interrogating thumb, the clank of the shod
    horses on the granite floor,
The carnival of sleighs, the clinking and shouted
    jokes and pelts of snowballs;
The hurrahs for popular favorites . . . . the fury of
    roused mobs,
The flap of the curtained litter—the sick man
    inside, borne to the hospital,
The meeting of enemies, the sudden oath, the
    blows and fall,
The excited crowd—the policeman with his star
    quickly working his passage to the centre of the
    crowd;
The impassive stones that receive and return so
    many echoes,
The souls moving along . . . . are they invisible
    while the least atom of the stones is visible?
What groans of overfed or half-starved who fall on
    the flags sunstruck or in fits,
What exclamations of women taken suddenly, who
    hurry home and give birth to babes,
What living and buried speech is always vibrating
    here . . . . what howls restrained by decorum,

Arrests of criminals, slights, adulterous offers
      made, acceptances, rejections with convex lips,
I mind them or the resonance of them . . . . I come
      again and again.

The big doors of the country-barn stand open and
      ready,
The dried grass of the harvest-time loads the slow-
      drawn wagon,
The clear light plays on the brown gray and green
      intertinged,
The armfuls are packed to the sagging mow:
I am there . . . . I help . . . . I came stretched atop of
      the load,
I felt its soft jolts . . . . one leg reclined on the other,
I jump from the crossbeams, and seize the clover
      and timothy,
And roll head over heels, and tangle my hair full of
      wisps.

Alone far in the wilds and mountains I hunt,
Wandering amazed at my own lightness and glee,
In the late afternoon choosing a safe spot to pass
      the night,
Kindling a fire and broiling the freshkilled game,
Soundly falling asleep on the gathered leaves, my
      dog and gun by my side.

The Yankee clipper is under her three skysails . . . .
    she cuts the sparkle and scud,
My eyes settle the land . . . . I bend at her prow or
    shout joyously from the deck.

The boatmen and clamdiggers arose early and
    stopped for me,
I tucked my trowser-ends in my boots and went
    and had a good time,
You should have been with us that day round the
    chowder-kettle.

I Saw the Marriage of the Trapper in the Open Air

I saw the marriage of the trapper in the open air in
    the far-west . . . . the bride was a red girl,
Her father and his friends sat near by crosslegged
    and dumbly smoking . . . . they had moccasins
    to their feet and large thick blankets hanging
    from their shoulders;
On a bank lounged the trapper . . . . he was dressed
    mostly in skins . . . . his luxuriant beard and
    curls protected his neck,
One hand rested on his rifle . . . . the other hand
    held firmly the wrist of the red girl,
She had long eyelashes . . . . her head was bare . . . .
    her coarse straight locks descended upon her
    voluptuous limbs and reached to her feet.

The runaway slave came to my house and stopped
    outside,
I heard his motions crackling the twigs of the
    woodpile,
Through the swung half-door of the kitchen I saw
    him limpsey and weak,
And went where he sat on a log, and led him in
    and assured him,
And brought water and filled a tub for his sweated
    body and bruised feet,

And gave him a room that entered from my own,
    and gave him some coarse clean clothes,
And remember perfectly well his revolving eyes
    and his awkwardness,
And remember putting plasters on the galls of his
    neck and ankles;
He staid with me a week before he was recuperated
    and passed north,
I had him sit next me at table . . . . my firelock
    leaned in the corner.

Twenty-eight young men bathe by the shore,
Twenty-eight young men, and all so friendly,
Twenty-eight years of womanly life, and all so
    lonesome.

She owns the fine house by the rise of the bank,
She hides handsome and richly drest aft the blinds
    of the window.

Which of the young men does she like the best?
Ah the homeliest of them is beautiful to her.

Where are you off to, lady? for I see you,
You splash in the water there, yet stay stock still in
    your room.

Dancing and laughing along the beach came the
    twenty-ninth bather,
The rest did not see her, but she saw them and
    loved them.

The beards of the young men glistened with wet, it
    ran from their long hair,
Little streams passed all over their bodies.

An unseen hand also passed over their bodies,
It descended tremblingly from their temples and
    ribs.

The young men float on their backs, their white
    bellies swell to the sun . . . . they do not ask
    who seizes fast to them,
They do not know who puffs and declines with
    pendant and bending arch,
They do not think whom they souse with spray.

The Butcher-Boy Puts Off His Killing-Clothes

The butcher-boy puts off his killing-clothes, or
    sharpens his knife at the stall in the market,
I loiter enjoying his repartee and his shuffle and
    breakdown.

Blacksmiths with grimed and hairy chests environ
    the anvil,
Each has his main-sledge . . . . they are all out . . . .
    there is a great heat in the fire.

From the cinder-strewed threshold I follow their
    movements,
The lithe sheer of their waists plays even with their
    massive arms,
Overhand the hammers roll—overhand so slow—
    overhand so sure,
They do not hasten, each man hits in his place.

The negro holds firmly the reins of his four horses
    . . . . the block swags underneath on its tied-
    over chain,
The negro that drives the huge dray of the
    stoneyard . . . . steady and tall he stands poised
    on one leg on the stringpiece,
His blue shirt exposes his ample neck and breast
    and loosens over his hipband,

His glance is calm and commanding . . . . he tosses
    the slouch of his hat away from his forehead,
The sun falls on his crispy hair and moustache . . . .
    falls on the black of his polish'd and perfect
    limbs.

I behold the picturesque giant and love him . . . .
    and I do not stop there,
I go with the team also.

In me the caresser of life wherever moving . . . .
    backward as well as forward slueing,
To niches aside and junior bending.

Oxen that rattle the yoke or halt in the shade, what
    is that you express in your eyes?
It seems to me more than all the print I have read
    in my life.

My tread scares the wood-drake and wood-duck
    on my distant and daylong ramble,
They rise together, they slowly circle around.
. . . . I believe in those winged purposes,
And acknowledge the red yellow and white
    playing within me,
And consider the green and violet and the tufted
    crown intentional;

And do not call the tortoise unworthy because she
     is not something else,
And the mockingbird in the swamp never studied
     the gamut, yet trills pretty well to me,
And the look of the bay mare shames silliness out
     of me.

The Wild Gander Leads His Flock through the Cool Night

The wild gander leads his flock through the cool
      night,
Ya-honk! he says, and sounds it down to me like
      an invitation;
The pert may suppose it meaningless, but I listen
      closer,
I find its purpose and place up there toward the
      November sky.

The sharphoofed moose of the north, the cat on the
      housesill, the chickadee, the prairie-dog,
The litter of the grunting sow as they tug at her
      teats,
The brood of the turkeyhen, and she with her
      halfspread wings,
I see in them and myself the same old law.

The press of my foot to the earth springs a
      hundred affections,
They scorn the best I can do to relate them.

I am enamoured of growing outdoors,
Of men that live among cattle or taste of the ocean
      or woods,
Of the builders and steerers of ships, of the
      wielders of axes and mauls, of the drivers of
      horses,

I can eat and sleep with them week in and week
out.

What is commonest and cheapest and nearest and
easiest is Me,
Me going in for my chances, spending for vast
returns,
Adorning myself to bestow myself on the first that
will take me,
Not asking the sky to come down to my goodwill,
Scattering it freely forever.

The Pure Contralto Sings in the Organloft

The pure contralto sings in the organloft,

The carpenter dresses his plank . . . . the tongue of
his foreplane whistles its wild ascending lisp,

The married and unmarried children ride home to
their thanksgiving dinner,

The pilot seizes the king-pin, he heaves down with
a strong arm,

The mate stands braced in the whaleboat, lance
and harpoon are ready,

The duck-shooter walks by silent and cautious
stretches,

The deacons are ordained with crossed hands at
the altar,

The spinning-girl retreats and advances to the
hum of the big wheel,

The farmer stops by the bars of a Sunday and looks
at the oats and rye,

The lunatic is carried at last to the asylum a
confirmed case,

He will never sleep any more as he did in the cot in
his mother's bedroom;

The jour printer with gray head and gaunt jaws
works at his case,

He turns his quid of tobacco, his eyes get blurred
with the manuscript;

The malformed limbs are tied to the anatomist's
table,

What is removed drops horribly in a pail;

The quadroon girl is sold at the stand . . . . the
drunkard nods by the barroom stove,

The machinist rolls up his sleeves . . . . the
policeman travels his beat . . . . the gatekeeper
marks who pass,

The young fellow drives the express-wagon I
love him though I do not know him;

The half-breed straps on his light boots to compete
in the race,

The western turkey-shooting draws old and young
. . . . some lean on their rifles, some sit on logs,

Out from the crowd steps the marksman and takes
his position and levels his piece;

The groups of newly-come immigrants cover the
wharf or levee,

The woollypates hoe in the sugarfield, the overseer
views them from his saddle;

The bugle calls in the ballroom, the gentlemen run
for their partners, the dancers bow to each
other;

The youth lies awake in the cedar-roofed garret
and harks to the musical rain,

The Wolverine sets traps on the creek that helps
fill the Huron,

The reformer ascends the platform, he spouts with
his mouth and nose,

The company returns from its excursion, the
    darkey brings up the rear and bears the well-
    riddled target,
The squaw wrapt in her yellow-hemmed cloth is
    offering moccasins and beadbags for sale,
The connoisseur peers along the exhibition-gallery
    with halfshut eyes bent sideways,
The deckhands make fast the steamboat, the plank
    is thrown for the shoregoing passengers,
The young sister holds out the skein, the elder
    sister winds it off in a ball and stops now and
    then for the knots,
The one-year wife is recovering and happy, a week
    ago she bore her first child,
The cleanhaired Yankee girl works with her
    sewing-machine or in the factory or mill,
The nine months' gone is in the parturition
    chamber, her faintness and pains are
    advancing;
The pavingman leans on his twohanded rammer—
    the reporter's lead flies swiftly over the
    notebook —the signpainter is lettering with red
    and gold,
The canal-boy trots on the towpath—the
    bookkeeper counts at his desk—the shoemaker
    waxes his thread,
The conductor beats time for the band and all the
    performers follow him,

The child is baptised—the convert is making the
      first professions,
The regatta is spread on the bay .... how the
      white sails sparkle!
The drover watches his drove, he sings out to them
      that would stray,
The pedlar sweats with his pack on his back—the
      purchaser higgles about the odd cent,
The camera and plate are prepared, the lady must
      sit for her daguerreotype,
The bride unrumples her white dress, the
      minutehand of the clock moves slowly,
The opium eater reclines with rigid head and just-
      opened lips,
The prostitute draggles her shawl, her bonnet bobs
      on her tipsy and pimpled neck,
The crowd laugh at her blackguard oaths, the men
      jeer and wink to each other,
(Miserable! I do not laugh at your oaths nor jeer
      you,)
The President holds a cabinet council, he is
      surrounded by the great secretaries,
On the piazza walk five friendly matrons with
      twined arms;
The crew of the fish-smack pack repeated layers of
      halibut in the hold,
The Missourian crosses the plains toting his wares
      and his cattle,

The fare-collector goes through the train—he gives
notice by the jingling of loose change,
The floormen are laying the floor—the tinners are
tinning the roof—the masons are calling for
mortar,
In single file each shouldering his hod pass onward
the laborers;
Seasons pursuing each other the indescribable
crowd is gathered . . . . it is the Fourth of July
. . . . what salutes of cannon and small arms!
Seasons pursuing each other the plougher ploughs
and the mower mows and the wintergrain falls
in the ground;
Off on the lakes the pikefisher watches and waits
by the hole in the frozen surface,
The stumps stand thick round the clearing, the
squatter strikes deep with his axe,
The flatboatmen make fast toward dusk near the
cottonwood or pekantrees,
The coon-seekers go now through the regions of
the Red river, or through those drained by the
Tennessee, or through those of the Arkansas,
The torches shine in the dark that hangs on the
Chattahoochee or Altamahaw;
Patriarchs sit at supper with sons and grandsons
and great grandsons around them,
In walls of adobe, in canvass tents, rest hunters and
trappers after their day's sport.

The city sleeps and the country sleeps,
The living sleep for their time . . . . the dead sleep
    for their time,
The old husband sleeps by his wife and the young
    husband sleeps by his wife;
And these one and all tend inward to me, and I
    tend outward to them,
And such as it is to be of these more or less I am.

I Am of Old and Young, of the Foolish as Much as the Wise

I am of old and young, of the foolish as much as
    the wise,
Regardless of others, ever regardful of others,
Maternal as well as paternal, a child as well as a
    man,
Stuffed with the stuff that is coarse, and stuffed
    with the stuff that is fine,
One of the great nation, the nation of many
    nations—the smallest the same and the largest
    the same,
A southerner soon as a northener, a planter
    nonchalant and hospitable,
A Yankee bound my own way . . . . ready for trade
    . . . . my joints the limberest joints on earth and
    the sternest joints on earth,
A Kentuckian walking the vale of the Elkhorn in
    my deerskin leggings,
A boatman over the lakes or bays or along coasts . . . .
    a Hoosier, a Badger, a Buckeye,
A Louisianian or Georgian, a poke-easy from
    sandhills and pines,
At home on Canadian snowshoes or up in the
    bush, or with fishermen off Newfoundland,
At home in the fleet of iceboats, sailing with the
    rest and tacking,
At home on the hills of Vermont or in the woods
    of Maine or the Texan ranch,

Comrade of Californians . . . . comrade of
    free northwesterners, loving their big
    proportions,
Comrade of raftsmen and coalmen—comrade
    of all who shake hands and welcome to
    drink and meat;
A learner with the simplest, a teacher of the
    thoughtfulest,
A novice beginning experient of myriads of
    seasons,
Of every hue and trade and rank, of every caste
    and religion,
Not merely of the New World but of Africa
    Europe or Asia . . . . a wandering savage,
A farmer, mechanic, or artist . . . . a gentleman,
    sailor, lover or quaker,
A prisoner, fancy-man, rowdy, lawyer, physician
    or priest.

I resist anything better than my own diversity,
And breathe the air and leave plenty after me,
And am not stuck up, and am in my place.

The moth and the fisheggs are in their place,
The suns I see and the suns I cannot see are in their
    place,
The palpable is in its place and the impalpable is in
    its place.

These are the thoughts of all men in all ages and
    lands, they are not original with me,
If they are not yours as much as mine they are
    nothing or next to nothing,
If they do not enclose everything they are next to
    nothing,
If they are not the riddle and the untying of the
    riddle they are nothing,
If they are not just as close as they are distant they
    are nothing.

This Is the Grass That Grows

This is the grass that grows wherever the land is
    and the water is,
This is the common air that bathes the globe.

This is the breath of laws and songs and behaviour,
This is the tasteless water of souls . . . . this is the
    true sustenance,
It is for the illiterate . . . . it is for the judges of the
    supreme court . . . . it is for the federal capitol
    and the state capitols,
It is for the admirable communes of literary men
    and composers and singers and lecturers and
    engineers and savans,
It is for the endless races of working people and
    farmers and seamen.

This is the trill of a thousand clear cornets and
    scream of the octave flute and strike of
    triangles.

I play not a march for victors only . . . . I play great
    marches for conquered and slain persons.

Have you heard that it was good to gain the day?
I also say it is good to fall . . . . battles are lost in the
    same spirit in which they are won.

I Sound Triumphal Drums for the Dead

I sound triumphal drums for the dead . . . . I fling
    through my embouchures the loudest and
    gayest music to them,
Vivas to those who have failed, and to those whose
    war-vessels sank in the sea, and those
    themselves who sank in the sea,
And to all generals that lost engagements, and all
    overcome heroes, and the numberless unknown
    heroes equal to the greatest heroes known.

This is the meal pleasantly set . . . . this is the meat
    and drink for natural hunger,
It is for the wicked just the same as the righteous . . . .
    I make appointments with all, I will not have a
    single person slighted or left away,
The keptwoman and sponger and thief are hereby
    invited . . . . the heavy-lipped slave is invited . . . .
    the venerealee is invited,
There shall be no difference between them and the
    rest.

This is the press of a bashful hand . . . . this is the
    float and odor of hair,
This is the touch of my lips to yours . . . . this is the
    murmur of yearning,

This is the far-off depth and height reflecting my
    own face,
This is the thoughtful merge of myself and the
    outlet again.

Do You Guess I Have Some Intricate Purpose?

Do you guess I have some intricate purpose?
Well I have . . . . for the April rain has, and the
    mica on the side of a rock has.

Do you take it I would astonish?
Does the daylight astonish? or the early redstart
    twittering through the woods?
Do I astonish more than they?

This hour I tell things in confidence,
I might not tell everybody but I will tell you.

Who goes there! hankering, gross, mystical, nude?
How is it I extract strength from the beef I eat?

What is a man anyhow? What am I? and what are
    you?
All I mark as my own you shall offset it with your
    own,
Else it were time lost listening to me.

I do not snivel that snivel the world over,
That months are vacuums and the ground but
    wallow and filth,
That life is a suck and a sell, and nothing remains
    at the end but threadbare crape and tears.

Whimpering and truckling fold with powders for
    invalids . . . . conformity goes to the fourth-
    removed,
I cock my hat as I please indoors or out.

Shall I pray? Shall I venerate and be ceremonious?

Divine Am I Inside and Out

Divine am I inside and out, and I make holy
    whatever I touch or am touched from;
The scent of these arm-pits is aroma finer than
    prayer,
This head is more than churches or bibles or
    creeds.

If I worship any particular thing it shall be some of
    the spread of my body;
Translucent mould of me it shall be you,
Shaded ledges and rests, firm masculine coulter, it
    shall be you,
Whatever goes to the tilth of me it shall be you,
You my rich blood, your milky stream pale
    strippings of my life;
Breast that presses against other breasts it shall be
    you,
My brain it shall be your occult convolutions,
Root of washed sweet-flag, timorous pond-snipe,
    nest of guarded duplicate eggs, it shall be you,
Mixed tussled hay of head and beard and brawn it
    shall be you,
Trickling sap of maple, fibre of manly wheat, it
    shall be you;
Sun so generous it shall be you,
Vapors lighting and shading my face it shall be
    you,
You sweaty brooks and dews it shall be you,

Winds whose soft-tickling genitals rub against me
    it shall be you,
Broad muscular fields, branches of liveoak, loving
    lounger in my winding paths, it shall be you,
Hands I have taken, face I have kissed, mortal I
    have ever touched, it shall be you.

I dote on myself . . . . there is that lot of me, and
    all so luscious,
Each moment and whatever happens thrills me
    with joy.

I cannot tell how my ankles bend . . . . nor whence
    the cause of my faintest wish,
Nor the cause of the friendship I emit . . . . nor the
    cause of the friendship I take again.

To walk up my stoop is unaccountable I
    pause to consider if it really be,
That I eat and drink is spectacle enough for the
    great authors and schools,
A morning-glory at my window satisfies me more
    than the metaphysics of books.

To behold the daybreak!
The little light fades the immense and diaphanous
    shadows,
The air tastes good to my palate.

Hefts of the moving world at innocent gambols,
    silently rising, freshly exuding,
Scooting obliquely high and low.

Something I cannot see puts upward libidinous
    prongs,
Seas of bright juice suffuse heaven.

The earth by the sky staid with . . . . the daily close
    of their junction,
The heaved challenge from the east that moment
    over my head,
The mocking taunt, See then whether you shall be
    master!

Dazzling and tremendous how quick the sunrise
    would kill me,
If I could not now and always send sunrise out of
    me.

We also ascend dazzling and tremendous as the
    sun,
We found our own my soul in the calm and cool of
    the daybreak.

All Truths Wait in All Things

All truths wait in all things,
They neither hasten their own delivery nor resist
    it,
They do not need the obstetric forceps of the
    surgeon,
The insignificant is as big to me as any,
What is less or more than a touch?

Logic and sermons never convince,
The damp of the night drives deeper into my soul.

Only what proves itself to every man and woman
    is so,
Only what nobody denies is so.

A minute and a drop of me settle my brain;
I believe the soggy clods shall become lovers and
    lamps,
And a compend of compends is the meat of a man
    or woman,
And a summit and flower there is the feeling they
    have for each other,
And they are to branch boundlessly out of that
    lesson until it becomes omnific,
And until every one shall delight us, and we them.

I believe a leaf of grass is no less than the
    journeywork of the stars,

And the pismire is equally perfect, and a grain of
   sand, and the egg of the wren,
And the tree-toad is a chef-d'ouvre for the highest,
And the running blackberry would adorn the
   parlors of heaven,
And the narrowest hinge in my hand puts to scorn
   all machinery,
And the cow crunching with depressed head
   surpasses any statue,
And a mouse is miracle enough to stagger
   sextillions of infidels,
And I could come every afternoon of my life to
   look at the farmer's girl boiling her iron tea-
   kettle and baking shortcake.

I find I incorporate gneiss and coal and long-
   threaded moss and fruits and grains and
   esculent roots,
And am stucco'd with quadrupeds and birds all
   over,
And have distanced what is behind me for good
   reasons,
And call any thing close again when I desire it.

In vain the speeding or shyness,
In vain the plutonic rocks send their old heat
   against my approach,

In vain the mastadon retreats beneath its own
    powdered bones,
In vain objects stand leagues off and assume
    manifold shapes,
In vain the ocean settling in hollows and the great
    monsters lying low,
In vain the buzzard houses herself with the sky,
In vain the snake slides through the creepers and
    logs,
In vain the elk takes to the inner passes of the
    woods,
In vain the razorbilled auk sails far north to
    Labrador,
I follow quickly . . . . I ascend to the nest in the
    fissure of the cliff.

I think I could turn and live awhile with the
    animals . . . . they are so placid and self-
    contained,
I stand and look at them sometimes half the day
    long.

They do not sweat and whine about their
    condition,
They do not lie awake in the dark and weep for
    their sins,
They do not make me sick discussing their duty to
    God,

Not one is dissatisfied . . . . not one is demented
    with the mania of owning things,
Not one kneels to another nor to his kind that
    lived thousands of years ago,
Not one is respectable or industrious over the
    whole earth.

So they show their relations to me and I accept
    them;
They bring me tokens of myself . . . . they evince
    them plainly in their possession.

I do not know where they got those tokens,
I must have passed that way untold times ago and
    negligently dropt them,
Myself moving forward then and now and forever,
Gathering and showing more always and with
    velocity,
Infinite and omnigenous and the like of these
    among them;
Not too exclusive toward the reachers of my
    remembrancers,
Picking out here one that shall be my amie,
Choosing to go with him on brotherly terms.

A gigantic beauty of a stallion, fresh and responsive
    to my caresses,
Head high in the forehead and wide between the
    ears,
Limbs glossy and supple, tail dusting the ground,
Eyes well apart and full of sparkling wickedness
    . . . . ears finely cut and flexibly moving.

His nostrils dilate . . . . my heels embrace him . . . .
    his well built limbs tremble with pleasure . . . .
    we speed around and return.

I but use you a moment and then I resign you
    stallion . . . . and do not need your paces, and
    outgallop them,
And myself as I stand or sit pass faster than you.

Who Learns My Lesson Complete?

Who learns my lesson complete?
Boss and journeyman and apprentice? . . . .
    churchman and atheist?
The stupid and the wise thinker . . . . parents and
    offspring . . . . merchant and clerk and porter
    and customer . . . . editor, author, artist and
    schoolboy?

Draw nigh and commence,
It is no lesson . . . . it lets down the bars to a good
    lesson,
And that to another . . . . and every one to another
    still.

The great laws take and effuse without argument,
I am of the same style, for I am their friend,
I love them quits and quits . . . . I do not halt and
    make salaams.

I lie abstracted and hear beautiful tales of things
    and the reasons of things,
They are so beautiful I nudge myself to listen.

I cannot say to any person what I hear I
    cannot say it to myself . . . . it is very wonderful.

It is no little matter, this round and delicious globe,
    moving so exactly in its orbit forever and ever,
    without one jolt or the untruth of a single second;

I do not think it was made in six days, nor in ten
    thousand years, nor ten decillions of years,
Nor planned and built one thing after another, as
    an architect plans and builds a house.

I do not think seventy years is the time of a man or
    woman,
Nor that seventy millions of years is the time of a
    man or woman,
Nor that years will ever stop the existence of me or
    any one else.

Is it wonderful that I should be immortal? as every
    one is immortal,
I know it is wonderful . . . . but my eyesight is
    equally wonderful . . . . and how I was
    conceived in my mother's womb is equally
    wonderful,
And how I was not palpable once but am now . . . .
    and was born on the last day of May 1819 . . . .
    and passed from a babe in the creeping trance
    of three summers and three winters to
    articulate and walk . . . . are all equally
    wonderful.

And that I grew six feet high . . . . and that I have
    become a man thirty-six years old in 1855 . . . .
    and that I am here anyhow—are all equally
    wonderful;

And that my soul embraces you this hour, and we
affect each other without ever seeing each
other, and never perhaps to see each other, is
every bit as wonderful:
And that I can think such thoughts as these is just
as wonderful,
And that I can remind you, and you think them
and know them to be true is just as wonderful,
And that the moon spins round the earth and on
with the earth is equally wonderful,
And that they balance themselves with the sun and
stars is equally wonderful.

Come I should like to hear you tell me what there
is in yourself that is not just as wonderful,
And I should like to hear the name of anything
between Sunday morning and Saturday night
that is not just as wonderful.

Great Are the Myths

Great are the myths . . . . I too delight in them,
Great are Adam and Eve . . . . I too look back and
    accept them;
Great the risen and fallen nations, and their poets,
    women, sages, inventors, rulers, warriors and
    priests.

Great is liberty! Great is equality! I am their
    follower,
Helmsmen of nations, choose your craft . . . . where
    you sail I sail,
Yours is the muscle of life or death . . . . yours is the
    perfect science . . . . in you I have absolute faith.

Great is today, and beautiful,
It is good to live in this age . . . . there never was
    any better.

Great are the plunges and throes and triumphs and
    falls of democracy,
Great the reformers with their lapses and screams,
Great the daring and venture of sailors on new
    explorations.

Great are yourself and myself,
We are just as good and bad as the oldest and
    youngest or any,

What the best and worst did we could do,
What they felt . . do not we feel it in ourselves?
What they wished . . do we not wish the same?

Great is youth, and equally great is old age . . . .
    great are the day and night;
Great is wealth and great is poverty . . . . great is
    expression and great is silence.

Youth large lusty and loving . . . . youth full of
    grace and force and fascination,
Do you know that old age may come after you
    with equal grace and force and fascination?

Day fullblown and splendid . . . . day of the
    immense sun, and action and ambition and
    laughter,
The night follows close, with millions of suns, and
    sleep and restoring darkness.

Wealth with the flush hand and fine clothes and
    hospitality:
But then the soul's wealth—which is candor and
    knowledge and pride and enfolding love:
Who goes for men and women showing poverty
    richer than wealth?

Expression of speech . . in what is written or said
    forget not that silence is also expressive,
That anguish as hot as the hottest and contempt as
    cold as the coldest may be without words,
That the true adoration is likewise without words
    and without kneeling.

Great is the greatest nation . . the nation of clusters
    of equal nations.

Great is the earth, and the way it became what it is,
Do you imagine it is stopped at this? . . . . and the
    increase abandoned?
Understand then that it goes as far onward from
    this as this is from the times when it lay in
    covering waters and gases.

Great is the quality of truth in man,
The quality of truth in man supports itself through
    all changes,
It is inevitably in the man . . . . He and it are in
    love, and never leave each other.

The truth in man is no dictum . . . . it is vital as
    eyesight,
If there be any soul there is truth . . . . if there be

man or woman there is truth . . . . If there be
  physical or moral there is truth,
If there be equilibrium or volition there is truth . . . . if
  there be things at all upon the earth there is truth.

O truth of the earth! O truth of things! I am
  determined to press the whole way toward you,
Sound your voice! I scale mountains or dive in the
  sea after you.

Great is language . . . . it is the mightiest of the
  sciences,
It is the fulness and color and form and diversity of
  the earth . . . . and of men and women . . . . and
  of all qualities and processes;
It is greater than wealth . . . . it is greater than
  buildings or ships or religions or paintings or
  music.

Great is the English speech . . . . What speech is so
  great as the English?
Great is the English brood . . . . What brood has so
  vast a destiny as the English?
It is the mother of the brood that must rule the
  earth with the new rule,
The new rule shall rule as the soul rules, and as the
  love and justice and equality that are in the soul
  rule.

Great is the law . . . . Great are the old few
    landmarks of the law . . . . they are the same in
    all times and shall not be disturbed.
Great are marriage, commerce, newspapers, books,
    freetrade, railroads, steamers, international
    mails and telegraphs and exchanges.

Great is Justice;
Justice is not settled by legislators and laws . . . . it
    is in the soul,
It cannot be varied by statutes any more than love
    or pride or the attraction of gravity can,
It is immutable . . it does not depend on majorities
    . . . . majorities or what not come at last before
    the same passionless and exact tribunal.

For justice are the grand natural lawyers and
    perfect judges . . . . it is in their souls,
It is well assorted . . . . they have not studied for
    nothing . . . . the great includes the less,
They rule on the highest grounds . . . . they oversee
    all eras and states and administrations,

The perfect judge fears nothing . . . . he could go
    front to front before God,
Before the perfect judge all shall stand back . . . .
    life and death shall stand back . . . . heaven and
    hell shall stand back.

Great is goodness;
I do not know what it is any more than I know
   what health is . . . . but I know it is great.

Great is wickedness . . . . I find I often admire it just
   as much as I admire goodness:
Do you call that a paradox? It certainly is a paradox.

The eternal equilibrium of things is great, and the
   eternal overthrow of things is great,
And there is another paradox.

Great is life . . and real and mystical . . wherever
   and whoever,
Great is death . . . . Sure as life holds all parts
   together, death holds all parts together;
Sure as the stars return again after they merge in
   the light, death is great as life.

Poems from *Leaves of Grass*
—the second edition (1856)

Poem of Wonder at The Resurrection of The Wheat (9)

Something startles me where I thought I was
   safest,
I withdraw from the still woods I loved,
I will not go now on the pastures to walk,
I will not strip my clothes from my body to meet
   my lover the sea,
I will not touch my flesh to the earth, as to other
   flesh, to renew me.

How can the ground not sicken of men?
How can you be alive, you growths of spring?
How can you furnish health, you blood of herbs,
   roots, orchards, grain?
Are they not continually putting distempered
   corpses in the earth?
Is not every continent worked over and over with
   sour dead?
Where have you disposed of those carcasses of the
   drunkards and gluttons of so many
   generations?
Where have you drawn off all the foul liquid and
   meat?
I do not see any of it upon you today—or perhaps I
   am deceived,
I will run a furrow with my plough—I will press
   my spade through the sod, and turn it up
   underneath,

I am sure I shall expose some of the foul meat.

Behold!
This is the compost of billions of premature
corpses,
Perhaps every mite has once formed part of a sick
person,
Yet Behold!
The grass covers the prairies,
The bean bursts noiselessly through the mould in
the garden,
The delicate spear of the onion pierces upward,
The apple-buds cluster together on the apple-
branches,
The resurrection of the wheat appears with pale
visage out of its graves,
The tinge awakes over the willow-tree and the
mulberry-tree,
The he-birds carol mornings and evenings, while
the she-birds sit on their nests,
The young of poultry break through the hatched
eggs,
The new-born of animals appear, the calf is dropt
from the cow, the colt from the mare,
Out of its little hill faithfully rise the potato's dark
green leaves,
Out of its hill rises the yellow maize-stalk;

The summer growth is innocent and disdainful
    above all those strata of sour dead.

What chemistry!
That the winds are really not infectious!
That this is no cheat, this transparent green-wash
    of the sea, which is so amorous after me!
That it is safe to allow it to lick my naked body all
    over with its tongues!
That it will not endanger me with the fevers that
    have deposited themselves in it!
That all is clean, forever and forever!
That the cool drink from the well tastes so good!
That blackberries are so flavorous and juicy!
That the fruits of the apple-orchard, and of the
    orange-orchard—that melons, grapes, peaches,
    plums, will none of them poison me!
That when I recline on the grass I do not catch
    any disease!
Though probably every spear of grass rises out of
    what was once a catching disease.

Now I am terrified at the earth! it is that calm and
    patient,
It grows such sweet things out of such corruptions,
It turns harmless and stainless on its axis, with
    such endless successions of diseased corpses,

It distils such exquisite winds out of such infused
     fetor,
It renews with such unwitting looks, its prodigal,
     annual, sumptuous crops,
It gives such divine materials to men, and accepts
     such leavings from them at last.

Faith Poem (20)

I need no assurances—I am a man who is pre-
    occupied of his own soul;
I do not doubt that whatever I know at a given
    time, there waits for me more which I do not
    know;

I do not doubt that from under the feet, and beside
    the hands and face I am cognizant of, are now
    looking faces I am not cognizant of—calm and
    actual faces;
I do not doubt but the majesty and beauty of the
    world is latent in any iota of the world;
I do not doubt there are realizations I have no idea
    of, waiting for me through time and through
    the universes—also upon this earth;

I do not doubt I am limitless, and that the
    universes are limitless—in vain I try to think
    how limitless;
I do not doubt that the orbs, and the systems of
    orbs, play their swift sports through the air on
    purpose—and that I shall one day be eligible to
    do as much as they, and more than they;

I do not doubt there is far more in trivialities,
    insects, vulgar persons, slaves, dwarfs, weeds,
    rejected refuse, than I have supposed;

I do not doubt there is more in myself than I have
supposed—and more in all men and women—
and more in my poems than I have supposed;

I do not doubt that temporary affairs keep on and
on, millions of years;
I do not doubt interiors have their interiors, and
exteriors have their exteriors—and that the
eye-sight has another eye-sight, and the hearing
another hearing, and the voice another voice;

I do not doubt that the passionately-wept deaths of
young men are provided for—and that the
deaths of young women, and the deaths of little
children, are provided for;
I do not doubt that wrecks at sea, no matter what
the horrors of them—no matter whose wife,
child, husband, father, lover, has gone down—
are provided for, to the minutest point;

I do not doubt that shallowness, meanness,
malignance, are provided for;
I do not doubt that cities, you, America, the
remainder of the earth, politics, freedom,
degradations, are carefully provided for;
I do not doubt that whatever can possibly happen,
any where, at any time, is provided for, in the
inherences of things.

Poem of Perfect Miracles (24)

Realism is mine, my miracles,
Take all of the rest—take freely—I keep but my
    own—I give only of them,
I offer them without end—I offer them to you
    wherever your feet can carry you, or your eyes
    reach.

Why! who makes much of a miracle?
As to me, I know of nothing else but miracles,
Whether I walk the streets of Manhattan,
Or dart my sight over the roofs of houses toward
    the sky,
Or wade with naked feet along the beach, just in
    the edge of the water,
Or stand under trees in the woods,
Or talk by day with any one I love—or sleep in the
    bed at night with any one I love,
Or sit at the table at dinner with my mother,
Or look at strangers opposite me riding in the car,
Or watch honey-bees busy around the hive, of an
    August forenoon,
Or animals feeding in the fields,
Or birds—or the wonderfulness of insects in the
    air,
Or the wonderfulness of the sun-down—or of stars
    shining so quiet and bright,
Or the exquisite, delicate, thin curve of the new-
    moon in May,

Or whether I go among those I like best, and that
like me best—mechanics, boatmen, farmers,
Or among the savans—or to the soiree—or to the
opera,
Or stand a long while looking at the movements of
machinery,
Or behold children at their sports,
Or the admirable sight of the perfect old man, or
the perfect old woman,
Or the sick in hospitals, or the dead carried to
burial,
Or my own eyes and figure in the glass,
These, with the rest, one and all, are to me
miracles,
The whole referring—yet each distinct and in its
place.

To me, every hour of the light and dark is a
miracle,
Every inch of space is a miracle,
Every square yard of the surface of the earth is
spread with the same,
Every cubic foot of the interior swarms with the
same;

Every spear of grass—the frames, limbs, organs, of
men and women, and all that concerns them,
All these to me are unspeakably perfect miracles.

To me the sea is a continual miracle,
The fishes that swim—the rocks—the motion of
     the waves—the ships, with men in them —
     what stranger miracles are there?

Poem of The Propositions of Nakedness (30)

Respondez! Respondez!

Let every one answer! Let all who sleep be waked! Let none evade—not you, any more than others!

Let that which stood in front go behind! and let that which was behind advance to the front and speak!

Let murderers, thieves, tyrants, bigots, unclean persons, offer new propositions!

Let the old propositions be postponed!

Let faces and theories be turned inside out! Let meanings be criminal as well as results! (Say! can results be criminal, and meanings not criminal?)

Let there be no suggestion besides the suggestion of drudgery!

Let none be pointed toward his destination! (Say! do you know your destination?)

Let trillions of men and women be mocked with bodies and mocked with souls!

Let the love that waits in them, wait! Let it die, or pass still-born to other spheres!

Let the sympathy that waits in every man, wait! or let it also pass, a dwarf, to other spheres!

Let contradictions prevail! Let one thing contradict another! and let one line of my poem contradict another!

Let the people sprawl with yearning aimless
    hands! Let their tongues be broken! Let their
    eyes be discouraged! Let none descend into
    their hearts with the fresh lusciousness of love!
Let the theory of America be management, caste,
    comparison! (Say! what other theory would you?)
Let them that distrust birth and death lead the
    rest! (Say! why shall they not lead you?)
Let the crust of hell be neared and trod on! Let the
    days be darker than the nights! Let slumber
    bring less slumber than waking-time brings!
Let the world never appear to him or her for
    whom it was all made!
Let the heart of the young man exile itself from the
    heart of the old man! and let the heart of the
    old man be exiled from that of the young man!
Let the sun and moon go! Let scenery take the
    applause of the audience! Let there be apathy
    under the stars!

Let freedom prove no man's inalienable right!
    Every one who can tyrannize, let him tyrannize
    to his satisfaction!
Let none but infidels be countenanced!
Let the eminence of meanness, treachery, sarcasm,
    hate, greed, indecency, impotence, lust, be
    taken for granted above all! Let poems, judges,
    governments, households, religions,

philosophies, take such for granted above all!
Let the worst men beget children out of the worst
women!
Let priests still play at immortality!
Let death be inaugurated!
Let nothing remain upon the earth except teachers,
artists, moralists, lawyers, and learned and
polite persons!
Let him who is without my poems be
assassinated!
Let the cow, the horse, the camel, the garden-bee—
Let the mud-fish, the lobster, the mussel, eel,
the sting-ray and the grunting pig-fish—Let
these, and the like of these, be put on a perfect
equality with man and woman!
Let churches accommodate serpents, vermin, and
the corpses of those who have died of the most
filthy of diseases!

Let marriage slip down among fools, and be for
none but fools!
Let men among themselves talk obscenely of
women! and let women among themselves talk
obscenely of men!
Let every man doubt every woman! and let every
woman trick every man!
Let us all, without missing one, be exposed in
public, naked, monthly, at the peril of our lives!

Let our bodies be freely handled and examined
by whoever chooses!
Let nothing but love-songs, pictures, statues,
elegant works, be permitted to exist upon the
earth!
Let the earth desert God, nor let there ever hence-
forth be mentioned the name of God!
Let there be no God!
Let there be money, business, railroads, imports,
exports, custom, authority, precedents, pallor,
dyspepsia, smut, ignorance, unbelief!
Let judges and criminals be transposed! Let the
prison-keepers be put in prison! Let those that
were prisoners take the keys! (Say! why might
they not just as well be transposed?)
Let the slaves be masters! Let the masters become
slaves!
Let the reformers descend from the stands where
they are forever bawling! Let an idiot or insane
person appear on each of the stands!

Let the Asiatic, the African, the European, the
American and the Australian, go armed against
the murderous stealthiness of each other! Let
them sleep armed! Let none believe in good-
will!
Let there be no living wisdom! Let such be scorned
and derided off from the earth!

Let a floating cloud in the sky—Let a wave of the
sea—Let one glimpse of your eye-sight upon
the landscape or grass—Let growing mint,
spinach, onions, tomatoes—Let these be
exhibited as shows at a great price for
admission!

Let all the men of These States stand aside for a
few smouchers! Let the few seize on what they
choose! Let the rest gawk, giggle starve, obey!

Let shadows be furnished with genitals! Let
substances be deprived of their genitals!

Let there be immense cities—but through any of
them, not a single poet, saviour, knower, lover!

Let the infidels of These States laugh all faith
away! If one man be found who has faith, let
the rest set upon him! Let them affright faith!
Let them destroy the power of breeding faith!

Let the she-harlots and the he-harlots be prudent!
Let them dance on, while seeming lasts! (O
seeming! seeming! seeming!)

Let the preachers recite creeds! Let the preachers
of creeds never dare to go meditate upon the
hills, alone, by day or by night! (If one ever
once dare, he is lost!)

Let insanity have charge of sanity!

Let books take the place of trees, animals, rivers,
clouds!

Let the portraits of heroes supersede heroes!
Let the manhood of man never take steps after
itself! Let it take steps after eunuchs, and after
consumptive and genteel persons!
Let the white person tread the black person under
his heel! (Say! which is trodden under heel,
after all?)
Let the reflections of the things of the world be
studied in mirrors! Let the things themselves
continue unstudied!
Let a man seek pleasure everywhere except in
himself! Let a woman seek happiness
everywhere except in herself! (Say! what real
happiness have you had one single time
through your whole life?)
Let the limited years of life do nothing for the
limitless years of death! (Say! what do you
suppose death will do, then?)

Burial Poem (32)

To think of time! to think through the
    retrospection!
To think of today, and the ages continued
    henceforward!

Have you guessed you yourself would not
    continue? Have you dreaded those earth-
    beetles?
Have you feared the future would be nothing to
    you?

Is today nothing? Is the beginningless past
    nothing?
If the future is nothing, they are just as surely
    nothing.

To think that the sun rose in the east! that men
    and women were flexible, real, alive! that every
    thing was alive!
To think that you and I did not see, feel, think, nor
    bear our part!
To think that we are now here, and bear our part!

Not a day passes, not a minute or second, without
    an accouchement!
Not a day passes, not a minute or second, without
    corpse!

The dull nights go over, and the dull days also,
The soreness of lying so much in bed goes
     over,
The physician, after long putting off, gives the
     silent and terrible look for an answer,
The children come hurried and weeping, and the
     brothers and sisters are sent for,
Medicines stand unused on the shelf—the
     camphor-smell has pervaded the rooms,
The faithful hand of the living does not desert the
     hand of the dying,
The twitching lips press lightly on the forehead of
     the dying,
The breath ceases and the pulse of the heart ceases,
The corpse stretches on the bed, and the living
     look upon it,
It is palpable as the living are palpable.

The living look upon the corpse with their eye-
     sight,
But without eye-sight lingers a different living, and
     looks curiously on the corpse.

To think that the rivers will come to flow, and the
     snow fall, and fruits ripen, and act upon others
     as upon us now—yet not act upon us!
To think of all these wonders of city and country,

and others taking great interest in them—and
we taking no interest in them!

To think how eager we are in building our houses!
To think others shall be just as eager, and we quite
indifferent!

I see one building the house that serves him a few
years, or seventy or eighty years at most,
I see one building the house that serves him longer
than that.

Slow-moving and black lines creep over the whole
earth—they never cease—they are the burial
lines,
He that was President was buried, and he that is
now President shall surely be buried.

Cold dash of waves at the ferry-wharf—posh and
ice in the river, half-frozen mud in the streets, a
gray discouraged sky overhead, the short last
daylight of December,
A hearse and stages, other vehicles give place—the
funeral of an old Broadway stage-driver, the
cortege mostly drivers.

Rapid the trot to the cemetery, duly rattles the
    death-bell, the gate is passed, the grave is halted
    at, the living alight, the hearse uncloses,
The coffin is lowered and settled, the whip is laid
    on the coffin, the earth is swiftly shovelled in—
    a minute, no one moves or speaks—it is done,
He is decently put away—is there anything more?

He was a good fellow, free-mouthed, quick-
    tempered, not bad-looking, able to take his own
    part, witty, sensitive to a slight, ready with life
    or death for a friend, fond of women, played
    some, ate hearty, drank hearty, had known
    what it was to be flush, grew low-spirited
    toward the last, sickened, was helped by a
    contribution, died aged forty-one years—and
    that was his funeral.

Thumb extended, finger uplifted, apron, cape,
    gloves, strap, wet-weather clothes, whip
    carefully chosen, boss, spotter, starter, hostler,
    somebody loafing on you, you loafing on
    somebody, head-way, man before and man
    behind, good day's work, bad day's work, pet
    stock, mean stock, first out, last out, turning in
    at night,

To think that these are so much and so nigh to
    other drivers—and he there takes no interest in
    them!

The markets, the government, the working-man's
    wages—to think what account they are
    through our nights and days!
To think that other working-men will make just as
    great account of them—yet we make little or
    no account!

The vulgar and the refined, what you call sin and
    what you call goodness—to think how wide a
    difference!
To think the difference will still continue to others,
    yet we lie beyond the difference!

To think how much pleasure there is!
Have you pleasure from looking at the sky? have
    you pleasure from poems?
Do you enjoy yourself in the city? or engaged in
    business? or planning a nomination and
    election? or with your wife and family?
Or with your mother and sisters? or in womanly
    house-work? or the beautiful maternal cares?
These also flow onward to others—you and I flow
    onward,

But in due time you and I shall take less interest in
    them.

Your farm, profits, crops—to think how engrossed
    you are!
To think there will still be farms, profits, crops—
    yet for you, of what avail?

What will be, will be well—for what is, is well,
To take interest is well, and not to take interest
    shall be well.

The sky continues beautiful, the pleasure of men
    with women shall never be sated, nor the
    pleasure of women with men, nor the pleasure
    from poems,
The domestic joys, the daily house-work or
    business, the building of houses—these are not
    phantasms, they have weight, form, location;
Farms, profits, crops, markets, wages, government,
    are none of them phantasms,
The difference between sin and goodness is no
    delusion,
The earth is not an echo—man and his life, and all
    the things of his life, are well-considered.

You are not thrown to the winds—you gather
    certainly and safely around yourself,
Yourself! Yourself! Yourself, forever and ever!

It is not to diffuse you that you were born of your
    mother and father—it is to identify you,
It is not that you should be undecided, but that you
    should be decided;
Something long preparing and formless is arrived
    and formed in you,
You are thenceforth secure, whatever comes or goes.

The threads that were spun are gathered, the weft
    crosses the warp, the pattern is systematic.

The preparations have every one been justified,
The orchestra have tuned their instruments
    sufficiently, the baton has given the signal.

The guest that was coming—he waited long for
    reasons—he is now housed,
He is one of those who are beautiful and happy—
    he is one of those that to look upon and be with
    is enough.

The law of the past cannot be eluded!
The law of the present and future cannot be eluded!

The law of the living cannot be eluded—it is eternal!
The law of promotion and transformation cannot
  be eluded!
The law of heroes and good-doers cannot be
  eluded!
The law of drunkards, informers, mean persons,
  cannot be eluded!

Slow-moving and black lines go ceaselessly over
  the earth,
Northerner goes carried, and southerner goes
  carried, and they on the Atlantic side, and they
  on the Pacific, and they between, and all
  through the Mississippi country, and all over
  the earth.

The great masters and kosmos are well as they
  go—the heroes and good-doers are well,
The known leaders and inventors, and the rich
  owners and pious and distinguished, may be
  well,
But there is more account than that—there is strict
  account of all.

The interminable hordes of the ignorant and
  wicked are not nothing,
The barbarians of Africa and Asia are not nothing,

The common people of Europe are not nothing—
    the American aborigines are not nothing,
The infected in the immigrant hospital are not
    nothing—the murderer or mean person is not
    nothing,
The perpetual successions of shallow people are not
    nothing as they go,
The prostitute is not nothing—the mocker of
    religion is not nothing as he goes.

I shall go with the rest—we have satisfaction,
I have dreamed that we are not to be changed so
    much, nor the law of us changed,
I have dreamed that heroes and good-doers shall
    be under the present and past law,
And that murderers, drunkards, liars, shall be
    under the present and past law,
For I have dreamed that the law they are under
    now is enough.

And I have dreamed that the satisfaction is not so
    much changed, and that there is no life without
    satisfaction;
What is the earth? what are body and soul,
    without satisfaction?

I shall go with the rest,
We cannot be stopped at a given point—that is no
    satisfaction,
To show us a good thing, or a few good things, for
    a space of time—that is no satisfaction,
We must have the indestructible breed of the best,
    regardless of time.

If otherwise, all these things came but to ashes of
    dung,
If maggots and rats ended us, then suspicion,
    treachery, death.
Do you suspect death? If I were to suspect death, I
    should die now,
Do you think I could walk pleasantly and well-
    suited toward annihilation?

Pleasantly and well-suited I walk,
Whither I walk I cannot define, but I know it is
    good,
The whole universe indicates that it is good,
The past and the present indicate that it is good.

How beautiful and perfect are the animals! How
    perfect is my soul!
How perfect the earth, and the minutest thing
    upon it!

What is called good is perfect, and what is called
    bad is just as perfect,
The vegetables and minerals are all perfect, and
    the imponderable fluids are perfect;
Slowly and surely they have passed on to this, and
    slowly and surely they yet pass on.

My soul! if I realize you, I have satisfaction,
Animals and vegetables! if I realize you, I have
    satisfaction,
Laws of the earth and air! if I realize you, I have
    satisfaction.

I cannot define my satisfaction, yet it is so,
I cannot define my life, yet it is so.

O I swear I think now that every thing has an
    eternal soul!
The trees have, rooted in the ground! the weeds of
    the sea have! the animals!

I swear I think there is nothing but immortality!
That the exquisite scheme is for it, and the
    nebulous float is for it, and the cohering is for it!
And all preparation is for it! and identity is for it!
    and life and death are for it!

Later Poems

I Hear America Singing

I hear America singing, the varied carols I hear,
Those of mechanics, each one singing his as it
    should be blithe and strong,
The carpenter singing his as he measures his plank
    or beam,
The mason singing his as he makes ready for
    work, or leaves off work,
The boatman singing what belongs to him in his
    boat, the deckhand singing on the steamboat
    deck,
The shoemaker singing as he sits on his bench, the
    hatter singing as he stands,
The wood-cutter's song, the ploughboy's on his
    way in the morning, or at noon intermission or
    at sundown,
The delicious singing of the mother, or of the
    young wife at work, or of the girl sewing or
    washing,
Each singing what belongs to him or her and to
    none else,
The day what belongs to the day—at night the
    party of young fellows, robust, friendly,
Singing with open mouths their strong melodious
    songs.

I Sing the Body Electric

I sing the body electric,
The armies of those I love engirth me and I
    engirth them,
They will not let me off till I go with them,
    respond to them,
And discorrupt them, and charge them full with
    the charge of the soul.

Was it doubted that those who corrupt their own
    bodies conceal themselves?
And if those who defile the living are as bad as
    they who defile the dead?
And if the body does not do fully as much as the
    soul?
And if the body were not the soul, what is the
    soul?

The love of the body of man or woman balks
    account, the body itself balks account,
That of the male is perfect, and that of the female
    is perfect.

The expression of the face balks account,
But the expression of a well-made man appears not
    only in his face,
It is in his limbs and joints also, it is curiously in
    the joints of his hips and wrists,

It is in his walk, the carriage of his neck, the flex of
   his waist and knees, dress does not hide him,
The strong sweet quality he has strikes through the
   cotton and broadcloth,
To see him pass conveys as much as the best poem,
   perhaps more,
You linger to see his back, and the back of his neck
   and shoulder-side.

The sprawl and fulness of babes, the bosoms and
   heads of women, the folds of their dress, their
   style as we pass in the street, the contour of
   their shape downwards,
The swimmer naked in the swimming-bath, seen
   as he swims through the transparent green-
   shine, or lies with his face up and rolls silently
   to and fro in the heave of the water,
The bending forward and backward of rowers in
   row-boats, the horseman in his saddle,
Girls, mothers, house-keepers, in all their
   performances,
The group of laborers seated at noon-time with their
   open dinner-kettles, and their wives waiting,
The female soothing a child, the farmer's daughter
   in the garden or cow-yard,
The young fellow hoeing corn, the sleigh-driver
   driving his six horses through the crowd,
The wrestle of wrestlers, two apprentice-boys,

quite grown, lusty, good-natured, native-born,
    out on the vacant lot at sundown after work,
The coats and caps thrown down, the embrace of
    love and resistance,
The upper-hold and under-hold, the hair rumpled
    over and blinding the eyes;
The march of firemen in their own costumes, the
    play of masculine muscle through clean-setting
    trowsers and waist-straps,
The slow return from the fire, the pause when the
    bell strikes suddenly again, and the listening on
    the alert,
The natural, perfect, varied attitudes, the bent
    head, the curv'd neck and the counting;
Such-like I love—I loosen myself, pass freely, am
    at the mother's breast with the little child,
Swim with the swimmers, wrestle with wrestlers,
    march in line with the firemen, and pause,
    listen, count.

I knew a man, a common farmer, the father of five
    sons,
And in them the fathers of sons, and in them the
    fathers of sons.

This man was of wonderful vigor, calmness, beauty
of person,
The shape of his head, the pale yellow and white of
his hair and beard, the immeasurable meaning
of his black eyes, the richness and breadth of
his manners,
These I used to go and visit him to see, he was wise
also,
He was six feet tall, he was over eighty years old,
his sons were massive, clean, bearded, tan-
faced, handsome,
They and his daughters loved him, all who saw
him loved him,
They did not love him by allowance, they loved
him with personal love,
He drank water only, the blood show'd like scarlet
through the clear-brown skin of his face,
He was a frequent gunner and fisher, he sail'd his
boat himself, he had a fine one presented to
him by a ship-joiner, he had fowling-pieces
presented to him by men that loved him,
When he went with his five sons and many grand-
sons to hunt or fish, you would pick him out as
the most beautiful and vigorous of the gang,
You would wish long and long to be with him, you
would wish to sit by him in the boat that you
and he might touch each other.

I have perceiv'd that to be with those I like is
    enough,
To stop in company with the rest at evening is
    enough,
To be surrounded by beautiful, curious, breathing,
    laughing flesh is enough,
To pass among them or touch any one, or rest my
    arm ever so lightly round his or her neck for a
    moment, what is this then?
I do not ask any more delight, I swim in it as in a sea.
There is something in staying close to men and
    women and looking on them, and in the
    contact and odor of them, that pleases the soul
    well,
All things please the soul, but these please the soul
    well.

This is the female form,
A divine nimbus exhales from it from head to foot,
It attracts with fierce undeniable attraction,
I am drawn by its breath as if I were no more than
    a helpless vapor, all falls aside but myself and it,
Books, art, religion, time, the visible and solid
    earth, and what was expected of heaven or
    fear'd of hell, are now consumed,
Mad filaments, ungovernable shoots play out of it,
    the response likewise ungovernable,

Hair, bosom, hips, bend of legs, negligent falling
    hands all diffused, mine too diffused,
Ebb stung by the flow and flow stung by the ebb,
    love-flesh swelling and deliciously aching,
Limitless limpid jets of love hot and enormous,
    quivering jelly of love, white-blow and
    delirious juice,
Bridegroom night of love working surely and
    softly into the prostrate dawn,
Undulating into the willing and yielding day,
Lost in the cleave of the clasping and sweet-flesh'd
    day.

This the nucleus—after the child is born of
    woman, man is born of woman,
This the bath of birth, this the merge of small and
    large, and the outlet again.

Be not ashamed women, your privilege encloses
    the rest, and is the exit of the rest,
You are the gates of the body, and you are the gates
    of the soul.
The female contains all qualities and tempers them,
She is in her place and moves with perfect balance,
She is all things duly veil'd, she is both passive and
    active,
She is to conceive daughters as well as sons, and
    sons as well as daughters.

As I see my soul reflected in Nature,
As I see through a mist, One with inexpressible
    completeness, sanity, beauty,
See the bent head and arms folded over the breast,
    the Female I see.

The male is not less the soul nor more, he too is in
    his place,
He too is all qualities, he is action and power,
The flush of the known universe is in him,
Scorn becomes him well, and appetite and defiance
    become him well,
The wildest largest passions, bliss that is utmost,
    sorrow that is utmost become him well, pride is
    for him,
The full-spread pride of man is calming and
    excellent to the soul,
Knowledge becomes him, he likes it always, he
    brings every thing to the test of himself,
Whatever the survey, whatever the sea and the sail
    he strikes soundings at last only here,
(Where else does he strike soundings except here?)

The man's body is sacred and the woman's body is
    sacred,
No matter who it is, it is sacred—is it the meanest
    one in the laborers' gang?

Is it one of the dull-faced immigrants just landed
    on the wharf?
Each belongs here or anywhere just as much as the
    well-off, just as much as you,
Each has his or her place in the procession.
(All is a procession,
The universe is a procession with measured and
    perfect motion.)

Do you know so much yourself that you call the
    meanest ignorant?
Do you suppose you have a right to a good sight,
    and he or she has no right to a sight?
Do you think matter has cohered together from its
    diffuse float, and the soil is on the surface, and
    water runs and vegetation sprouts,
For you only, and not for him and her?

A man's body at auction,
(For before the war I often go to the slave-mart
    and watch the sale,)
I help the auctioneer, the sloven does not half
    know his business.

Gentlemen look on this wonder,
Whatever the bids of the bidders they cannot be
    high enough for it,

For it the globe lay preparing quintillions of years
    without one animal or plant,
For it the revolving cycles truly and steadily roll'd.

In this head the all-baffling brain,
In it and below it the makings of heroes.

Examine these limbs, red, black, or white, they are
    cunning in tendon and nerve,
They shall be stript that you may see them.

Exquisite senses, life-lit eyes, pluck, volition,
Flakes of breast-muscle, pliant backbone and neck,
    flesh not flabby, good-sized arms and legs,
And wonders within there yet.

Within there runs blood,
The same old blood! the same red-running blood!
There swells and jets a heart, there all passions,
    desires, reachings, aspirations,
(Do you think they are not there because they are
    not express'd in parlors and lecture-rooms?)

This is not only one man, this the father of those
    who shall be fathers in their turns,
In him the start of populous states and rich
    republics,

Of him countless immortal lives with countless
    embodiments and enjoyments.

How do you know who shall come from the
    offspring of his offspring through the
    centuries?
(Who might you find you have come from
    yourself, if you could trace back through the
    centuries?)

A woman's body at auction,
She too is not only herself, she is the teeming
    mother of mothers,
She is the bearer of them that shall grow and be
    mates to the mothers.

Have you ever loved the body of a woman?
Have you ever loved the body of a man?
Do you not see that these are exactly the same to all
    in all nations and times all over the earth?

If any thing is sacred the human body is sacred,
And the glory and sweet of a man is the token of
    manhood untainted,
And in man or woman a clean, strong, firm-fibred
    body, is more beautiful than the most beautiful
    face.

Have you seen the fool that corrupted his own live
    body? or the fool that corrupted her own live
    body?
For they do not conceal themselves, and cannot
    conceal themselves.

O my body! I dare not desert the likes of you in
    other men and women, nor the likes of the
    parts of you,
I believe the likes of you are to stand or fall with
    the likes of the soul, (and that they are the soul,)
I believe the likes of you shall stand or fall with my
    poems, and that they are my poems,
Man's, woman's, child's, youth's, wife's, husband's,
    mother's, father's, young man's, young woman's
    poems,
Head, neck, hair, ears, drop and tympan of the ears,
Eyes, eye-fringes, iris of the eye, eyebrows, and the
    waking or sleeping of the lids,
Mouth, tongue, lips, teeth, roof of the mouth, jaws,
    and the jaw-hinges,
Nose, nostrils of the nose, and the partition,
Cheeks, temples, forehead, chin, throat, back of the
    neck, neck-slue,
Strong shoulders, manly beard, scapula, hind-
    shoulders, and the ample side-round of the
    chest,

Upper-arm, armpit, elbow-socket, lower-arm, arm-
    sinews, arm-bones,
Wrist and wrist-joints, hand, palm, knuckles,
    thumb, forefinger, finger-joints, finger-nails,
Broad breast-front, curling hair of the breast,
    breast-bone, breast-side,
Ribs, belly, backbone, joints of the backbone,
Hips, hip-sockets, hip-strength, inward and
    outward round, man-balls, man-root,
Strong set of thighs, well carrying the trunk above,
Leg-fibres, knee, knee-pan, upper-leg, under-leg,
Ankles, instep, foot-ball, toes, toe-joints, the heel;
All attitudes, all the shapeliness, all the belongings
    of my or your body or of any one's body, male
    or female,
The lung-sponges, the stomach-sac, the bowels
    sweet and clean,
The brain in its folds inside the skull-frame,
Sympathies, heart-valves, palate-valves, sexuality,
    maternity,
Womanhood, and all that is a woman, and the man
    that comes from woman,
The womb, the teats, nipples, breast-milk, tears,
    laughter, weeping, love-looks, love-
    perturbations and risings,
The voice, articulation, language, whispering,
    shouting aloud,

Food, drink, pulse, digestion, sweat, sleep,
 walking, swimming,
Poise on the hips, leaping, reclining, embracing,
 arm-curving and tightening,
The continual changes of the flex of the mouth,
 and around the eyes,
The skin, the sunburnt shade, freckles, hair,
The curious sympathy one feels when feeling with
 the hand the naked meat of the body,
The circling rivers the breath, and breathing it in
 and out,
The beauty of the waist, and thence of the hips,
 and thence downward toward the knees,
The thin red jellies within you or within me, the
 bones and the marrow in the bones,
The exquisite realization of health;
O I say these are not the parts and poems of the
 body only, but of the soul,
O I say now these are the soul!

Excerpts from Whitman's Prose Mystic Writings

Preface to the First Edition of *Leaves of Grass*

[*Note to readers:* This monumental preface to the simple poems that followed it is so bursting with ideas that it would be irresponsible to summarize it. Whitman clearly had a lot to say—and it needed to be said in mid-nineteenth century America, and perhaps still today.

These paragraphs are our best introduction to Whitman's poetics, his theory of how poems have meaning and what value poetry has in the world. Some of the ideas presented here were later turned into poetic lines for future editions of *Leaves of Grass*.]

America does not repel the past or what it has produced under its forms or amid other politics or the idea of castes or the old religions ... accepts the lesson with calmness ... is not so impatient as has been supposed that the slough still sticks to opinions and manners and literature while the life which served its requirements has passed into the new life of the new forms ... perceives that the corpse is slowly borne from the eating and sleeping rooms of the house ... perceives that it waits a little while in the door ... that it was fittest for its days ... that its action has descended to the stalwart and wellshaped heir who approaches ... and that he shall be fittest for his days.

The Americans of all nations at any time upon the earth have probably the fullest poetical nature. The

United States themselves are essentially the greatest poem. In the history of the earth hitherto the largest and most stirring appear tame and orderly to their ampler largeness and stir. Here at last is something in the doings of man that corresponds with the broadcast doings of the day and night. Here is not merely a nation but a teeming nation of nations. Here is action untied from strings necessarily blind to particulars and details magnificently moving in vast masses. Here is the hospitality which forever indicates heroes .... Here are the roughs and beards and space and ruggedness and nonchalance that the soul loves. Here the performance disdaining the trivial unapproached in the tremendous audacity of its crowds and groupings and the push of its perspective spreads with crampless and flowing breadth and showers its prolific and splendid extravagance. One sees it must indeed own the riches of the summer and winter, and need never be bankrupt while corn grows from the ground or the orchards drop apples or the bays contain fish or men beget children upon women.

Other states indicate themselves in their deputies .... but the genius of the United States is not best or most in its executives or legislatures, nor in its ambassadors or authors or colleges or churches or parlors, nor even in its newspapers or inventors ... but always most in the common people. Their manners speech dress friendships—the freshness and candor of their physiognomy—the picturesque looseness of their carriage ... their deathless attachment to freedom—their aversion to anything indecorous or soft or mean—the practical acknowledgment of the citizens of one state by the citizens of all other states—the fierceness of their roused resentment—their curiosity and welcome of novelty—their self-esteem and wonderful sympathy—their susceptibility to a slight—the air they have of persons who never knew how it felt to stand in the presence of superiors—the fluency of their speech—their delight in music, the sure symptom of manly tenderness and native elegance of soul ... their good temper and open handedness—the terrible significance of their elections—the President's taking off his hat to them, not they to him—these too are unrhymed poetry. It awaits the gigantic and generous treatment worthy of it.

The largeness of nature or the nation were monstrous without a corresponding largeness and generosity of the spirit of the citizen. Not nature nor swarming states nor streets and steamships nor prosperous business nor farms nor capital nor learning may suffice for the ideal of man ... nor suffice the poet. No reminiscences may suffice either. A live nation can always cut a deep mark and can have the best authority the cheapest ... namely from its own soul. This is the sum of the profitable uses of individuals or states and of present action and grandeur and of the subjects of poets.—As if it were necessary to trot back generation after generation to the eastern records! As if the beauty and sacredness of the demonstrable must fall behind that of the mythical! As if men do not make their mark out of any times! As if the opening of the western continent by discovery and what has transpired since in North and South America were less than the small theatre of the antique or the aimless sleepwalking of the middle ages! The pride of the United States leaves the wealth and finesse of the cities and all returns of commerce and agriculture and all the magnitude of geography or shows of exterior victory to enjoy the breed of full sized men or one full sized man unconquerable and simple....

The known universe has one complete lover and that is the greatest poet. He consumes an eternal passion and is indifferent which chance happens and which possible contingency of fortune or misfortune and persuades daily and hourly his delicious pay. What baulks or breaks others is fuel for his burning progress to contact and amorous joy. Other proportions of the reception of pleasure dwindle to nothing to his proportions. All expected from heaven or from the highest he is rapport with in the sight of the daybreak or a scene of the winter woods or the presence of children playing or with his arm round the neck of a man or woman. His love above all love has leisure and expanse ... he leaves room ahead of himself. He is no irresolute or suspicious lover ... he is sure ... he scorns intervals. His experience and the showers and thrills are not for nothing. Nothing can jar him ... suffering and darkness cannot—death and fear cannot. To him complaint and jealousy and envy are corpses buried and rotten in the earth ... he saw them buried. The sea is not surer of the shore or the shore of the sea than he is of the fruition of his love and of all perfection and beauty.

The fruition of beauty is no chance of hit or miss ... it is inevitable as life ... it is as exact and plumb as gravitation. From the eyesight proceeds another eyesight and from the hearing proceeds another hearing and from the voice proceeds another voice eternally curious of the harmony of things with man. To these respond perfections not only in the committees that were supposed to stand for the rest but in the rest themselves just the same. These understand the law of perfection in masses and floods ... that its finish is to each for itself and onward from itself ... that it is profuse and impartial ... that there is not a minute of the light or dark nor an acre of the earth and sea without it—nor any direction of the sky nor any trade or employment nor any turn of events. This is the reason that about the proper expression of beauty there is precision and balance ... one part does not need to be thrust above another. The best singer is not the one who has the most lithe and powerful organ ... the pleasure of poems is not in them that take the handsomest measure and similes and sound.

Without effort and without exposing in the least how it is done the greatest poet brings the spirit of any or all events and passions and scenes and persons some more and some less to bear on your individual character as you hear or read. To do this well is to compete with the laws that pursue and follow time. What is the purpose must surely be there and the clue of it must be there .... and the faintest indication is the indication of the best and then becomes the clearest indication. Past and present and future are not disjoined but joined. The greatest poet forms the consistence of what is to be from what has been and is. He drags the dead out of their coffins and stands them again on their feet .... he says to the past, Rise and walk before me that I may realize you. He learns the lesson .... he places himself where the future becomes present. The greatest poet does not only dazzle his rays over character and scenes and passions ... he finally ascends and finishes all ... he exhibits the pinnacles that no man can tell what they are for or what is beyond .... he glows a moment on the extremest verge. He is most wonderful in his last half-hidden smile or frown ... by that flash of the moment of parting the one that sees it shall be encouraged or terrified afterward for many years. The greatest poet does not moralize or make applications of morals ... he knows the soul. The soul has that measureless pride which consists in never acknowledging any lessons but its own. But it has sympathy as measureless as its pride and the one balances the other and neither can stretch too far while it stretches in company with the other. The inmost secrets of art sleep with the twain. The greatest poet has lain close betwixt both and they are vital in his style and thoughts.

The art of art, the glory of expression and the sunshine of the light of letters is simplicity. Nothing is better than simplicity .... nothing can make up for excess or for the lack of definiteness. To carry on the heave of impulse and pierce intellectual depths and give all subjects their articulations are powers neither common nor very uncommon. But to speak in literature with the perfect rectitude and insouciance of the movements of animals and the unimpeachableness of the sentiment of trees in the woods and grass by the roadside is the flawless triumph of art. If you have looked on him who has achieved it you have looked on one of the masters of the artists of all nations and times. You shall not contemplate the flight of the graygull over the bay or the mettlesome action of the blood horse or the tall leaning of sunflowers on their stalk or the appearance of the sun journeying through heaven or the appearance of the moon afterward with any more satisfaction than you shall contemplate him. The greatest poet has less a marked style and is more the channel of thoughts and things without increase or diminution and is the free channel of himself. He swears to his art, I will not be meddlesome, I will not have in my writing any elegance or effect or originality to hang in the way between me and the rest like curtains. I will have nothing hang in the way, not the richest curtains. What I tell I tell for precisely what it is. Let who may exalt or startle or fascinate or sooth I will have purposes as health or heat or snow has and be as regardless of observation. What I experience or portray shall go from my composition without a shred of my composition. You shall stand by my side and look in the mirror with me.

Open Letter to Ralph Waldo Emerson (1856)

Brooklyn, August, 1856

Here are thirty-two Poems [*Leaves of Grass*, second edition], which I send you, dear Friend and Master, not having found how I could satisfy myself with sending any usual acknowledgment of your letter. The first edition, on which you mailed me that till now unanswered letter, was twelve poems—I printed a thousand copies, and they readily sold; these thirty-two Poems I stereotype, to print several thousand copies of. I much enjoy making poems. Other work I have set for myself to do, to meet people and The States face to face, to confront them with an American rude tongue; but the work of my life is making poems. I keep on till I make a hundred, and then several hundred—perhaps a thousand. The way is clear to me. A few years, and the average annual call for my Poems is ten or twenty thousand copies—more, quite likely. Why should I hurry or compromise? In poems or in speeches I say the word or two that has got to be said, adhere to the body, step with the countless common footsteps, and remind every man and woman of something.

Master, I am a man who has perfect faith. Master, we have not come through centuries, caste, heroisms, fables, to halt in this land today. Or I think it is to collect a ten-fold impetus that any halt is made. As nature, inexorable, onward, resistless, impassive amid the threats and screams of disputants, so America. Let all defer. Let all attend respectfully the leisure of These States, their politics, poems, literature, manners, and their free-handed modes of training their own offspring. Their own comes, just matured, certain, numerous and capable enough, with egotistical tongues, with sinewed wrists, seizing openly what belongs to them. They resume Personality, too long left out of mind. Their shadows are projected in employments, in books, in the cities, in trade; their feet are on the flights of the steps of the Capitol; they dilate, a larger, brawnier, more candid, more democratic, lawless, positive native to The States, sweet-bodied, completer, dauntless, flowing, masterful, beard-faced, new race of men.

Swiftly, on limitless foundations, the United States too are founding a literature. It is all as well done, in my opinion, as could be practicable. Each element here is in condition. Every day I go among the people of Manhattan Island, Brooklyn, and other cities, and among the young men, to discover the spirit of them, and to refresh myself. These are to be attended to; I am myself more drawn here than to those authors, publishers, importations, reprints, and so forth. I pass coolly through those, understanding them perfectly well, and that they do the indispensable service, outside of men like me, which nothing else could do. In poems, the young men of The States shall be represented, for they out-rival the best of the rest of the earth.

The lists of ready-made literature which America inherits by the mighty inheritance of the English language—all the rich repertoire of traditions, poems, historics, metaphysics, plays, classics, translations, have made, and still continue, magnificent preparations for that other plainly signified literature, to be our own, to be electric, fresh, lusty, to express the full-sized body, male and female—to give the modern meanings of things, to grow up beautiful, lasting, commensurate with America, with all the passions of home, with the inimitable sympathies of having been boys and girls together, and of parents who were with our parents.

What else can happen The States, even in their own despite? That huge English flow, so sweet, so undeniable, has done incalculable good here, and is to be spoken of for its own sake with generous praise and with gratitude. Yet the price The States have had to lie under for the same has not been a small price. Payment prevails; a nation can never take the issues of the needs of other nations for nothing. America, grandest of lands in the theory of its politics, in popular reading, in hospitality, breadth, animal beauty, cities, ships, machines, money, credit, collapses quick as lightning at the repeated, admonishing, stern words, Where are any mental expressions from you, beyond what you have copied or stolen? Where the born throngs of poets, literats, orators, you promised? Will you but tag after other nations? They struggled long for their literature, painfully working their way, some with deficient languages, some with priest-craft, some in the endeavor just to live—yet achieved for their times, works, poems, perhaps the only solid consolation left to them through ages afterward of shame and decay. You are young, have the perfectest of dialects, a free press, a free government, the world forwarding its best to be with you. As justice has been strictly done to you, from this hour do strict justice to yourself. Strangle the singers who will not sing you loud and strong. Open the doors of The West. Call for new great masters to comprehend new arts, new perfections, new wants. Submit to the most robust bard till he remedy your barrenness. Then you will not need to adopt the heirs of others; you will have true heirs, begotten of yourself, blooded with your own blood.

With composure I see such propositions, seeing more and more every day of the answers that serve. Expressions do not yet serve, for sufficient reasons; but that is getting ready, beyond what the earth has hitherto known, to take home the expressions when they come, and to identify them with the populace of The States, which is the schooling cheaply procured by any outlay any number of years. Such schooling The States extract from the swarms of reprints, and from the current authors and editors. Such service and extract are done after enormous, reckless, free modes, characteristic of The States. Here are to be attained results never elsewhere thought possible; the modes are very grand too. The instincts of the American people are all perfect, and tend to make heroes. It is a rare thing in a man here to understand The States.

All current nourishments to literature serve. Of authors and editors I do not know how many there are in The States, but there are thousands, each one building his or her step to the stairs by which giants shall mount. Of the twenty-four modern mammoth two-double, three-double, and four-double cylinder presses now in the world, printing by steam, twenty-one of them are in These States. The twelve thousand large and small shops for dispensing books and newspapers—the same number of public libraries, any one of which has all the reading wanted to equip a man or woman for American reading—the three thousand different newspapers, the nutriment of the imperfect ones coming in just as usefully as any—the story papers, various, full of strong-flavored romances, widely circulated—the one-cent and two-cent journals—the political ones, no matter what side—the weeklies in the country—the sporting and pictorial papers—the monthly magazines, with plentiful imported feed—the sentimental novels, numberless copies of them—the low-priced flaring tales, adventures, biographies—all are prophetic; all waft rapidly on. I see that they swell wide, for reasons. I am not troubled at the movement of them, but greatly pleased. I see plying shuttles, the active ephemeral myriads of books also, faithfully weaving the garments of a generation of men, and a generation of women, they do not perceive or know. What a progress popular reading and writing has made in fifty years! What a progress fifty years hence! The time is at hand when inherent literature will be a main part of These States, as general and real as steam-power, iron, corn, beef, fish. First-rate American persons are to be supplied. Our perennial materials for fresh thoughts, histories, poems, music, orations, religions, recitations, amusements, will then not be disregarded, any more than our perennial fields, mines, rivers, seas. Certain things are established, and are immovable; in those things millions of years stand justified. The mothers and fathers of whom modern centuries have come, have not existed for nothing; they too had brains and hearts. Of course all literature, in all nations and years, will share marked attributes in common, as we all, of all ages, share the common human attributes. America is to be kept coarse and broad. What is to be done is to withdraw from precedents, and be directed to men and women—also to The States in their federalness; for the union of the parts of the body is not more necessary to their life than the union of These States is to their life.

A profound person can easily know more of the people than they know of themselves. Always waiting untold in the souls of the armies of common people, is stuff better than anything that can possibly appear in the leadership of the same. That gives final verdicts. In every department of These States, he who travels with a coterie, or with selected persons, or with imitators, or with infidels, or with the owners of slaves, or with that which is ashamed of the body of a man, or with that which is ashamed of the body of a woman, or with any thing less than the bravest and the openest, travels straight for the slopes of dissolution. The genius of all foreign literature is clipped and cut small, compared to our genius, and is essentially insulting to our usages, and to the organic compacts of These States. Old forms, old poems, majestic and proper in their own lands here in this land are exiles; the air here is very strong. Much that stands well and has a little enough place provided for it in the small scales of European kingdoms, empires, and the like, here stands haggard, dwarfed, ludicrous, or has no place little enough provided for it. Authorities, poems, models, laws, names, imported into America, are useful to America today to destroy them, and so move disencumbered to great works, great days.

Just so long, in our country or any country, as no revolutionists advance, and are backed by the people, sweeping off the swarms of routine representatives, officers in power, book-makers, teachers, ecclesiastics, politicians, just so long, I perceive, do they who are in power fairly represent that country, and remain of use, probably of very great use. To supersede them, when it is the pleasure of These States, full provision is made; and I say the time has arrived to use it with a strong hand. Here also the souls of the armies have not only overtaken the souls of the officer, but passed on, and left the souls of the officers behind out of sight many weeks' journey; and the souls of the armies now go en-masse without officers. Here also formulas, glosses, blanks, minutiæ, are choking the throats of the spokesmen to death. Those things most listened for, certainly those are the things least said.

There is not a single History of the World. There is not one of America, or of the organic compacts of These States, or of Washington, or of Jefferson, nor of Language, nor any Dictionary of the English Language. There is no great author; every one has demeaned himself to some etiquette or some impotence. There is no manhood or life-power in poems; there are shoats and geldings more like. Or literature will be dressed up, a fine gentleman, distasteful to our instincts, foreign to our soil. Its neck bends right and left wherever it goes. Its costumes and jewelry prove how little it knows Nature. Its flesh is soft; it shows less and less of the indefinable hard something that is Nature. Where is any thing but the shaved Nature of synods and schools? Where is a savage and luxuriant man? Where is an overseer? In lives, in poems, in codes of law, in Congress, in tuitions, theatres, conversations, argumentations, not a single head lifts itself clean out, with proof that it is their master, and has subordinated them to itself, and is ready to try their superiors. None believes in These States, boldly illustrating them in himself. Not a man faces round at the rest with terrible negative voice, refusing all terms to be bought off from his own eye-sight, or from the soul that he is, or from friendship, or from the body that he is, or from the soil and sea. To creeds, literature, art, the army, the navy, the executive, life is hardly proposed, but the sick and dying are proposed to cure the sick and dying. The churches are one vast lie; the people do not believe them, and they do not believe themselves; the priests are continually telling what they know well enough is not so, and keeping back what they know is so. The spectacle is a pitiful one. I think there can never be again upon the festive earth more bad-disordered persons deliberately taking seats, as of late in These States, at the heads of the public tables—such corpses' eyes for judges—such a rascal and thief in the Presidency.

Up to the present, as helps best, the people, like a lot of large boys, have no determined tastes, are quite unaware of the grandeur of themselves, and of their destiny, and of their immense strides—accept with voracity whatever is presented them in novels, histories, newspapers, poems, schools, lectures, every thing. Pretty soon, through these and other means, their development makes the fibre that is capable of itself, and will assume determined tastes. The young men will be clear what they want, and will have it. They will follow none except him whose spirit leads them in the like spirit with themselves. Any such man will be welcome as the flowers of May. Others will be put out without ceremony. How much is there anyhow, to the young men of These States, in a parcel of helpless dandies, who can neither fight, work, shoot, ride, run, command—some of them devout, some quite insane, some castrated—all second-hand, or third, fourth, or fifth hand—waited upon by waiters, putting not this land first, but always other lands first, talking of art, doing the most ridiculous things for fear of being called ridiculous, smirking and skipping along, continually taking off their hats—no one behaving, dressing, writing, talking, loving, out of any natural and manly tastes of his own, but each one looking cautiously to see how the rest behave, dress, write, talk, love—pressing the noses of dead books upon themselves and upon their country—favoring no poets, philosophs, literats here, but dog-like danglers at the heels of the poets, philosophs, literats, of enemies' lands—favoring mental expressions, models of gentlemen and ladies, social habitudes in These States, to grow up in sneaking defiance of the popular substratums of The States? Of course they and the likes of them can never justify the strong poems of America. Of course no feed of theirs is to stop and be made welcome to muscle the bodies, male and female, for Manhattan Island, Brooklyn, Boston, Worcester, Hartford, Portland, Montreal, Detroit, Buffalo, Cleveland, Milwaukee, St. Louis, Indianapolis, Chicago, Cincinnati, Iowa City, Philadelphia, Baltimore, Raleigh, Savannah, Charleston, Mobile, New Orleans, Galveston, Brownsville, San Francisco, Havana, and a thousand equal cities, present and to come. Of course what they and the likes of them have been used for, draws toward its close, after which they will all be discharged, and not one of them will ever be heard of any more.

America, having duly conceived, bears out of herself offspring of her own to do the workmanship wanted. To freedom, to strength, to poems, to personal greatness, it is never permitted to rest, not a generation or part of a generation. To be ripe beyond further increase is to prepare to die. The architects of These States laid their foundations, and passed to further spheres. What they laid is a work done; as much more remains. Now are needed other architects, whose duty is not less difficult, but perhaps more difficult. Each age forever needs architects. America is not finished, perhaps never will be; now America is a divine true sketch. There are Thirty-Two States sketched—the population thirty millions. In a few years there will be Fifty States. Again in a few years there will be A Hundred States, the population hundreds of millions, the freshest and freest of men. Of course such men stand to nothing less than the freshest and freest expression.

Poets here, literats here, are to rest on organic different bases from other countries; not a class set apart, circling only in the circle of themselves, modest and pretty, desperately scratching for rhymes, pallid with white paper, shut off, aware of the old pictures and traditions of the race, but unaware of the actual race around them—not breeding in and in among each other till they all have the scrofula. Lands of ensemble, bards of ensemble! Walking freely out from the old traditions, as our politics has walked out, American poets and literats recognize nothing behind them superior to what is present with them—recognize with joy the sturdy living forms of the men and women of These States, the divinity of sex, the perfect eligibility of the female with the male, all The States, liberty and equality, real articles, the different trades, mechanics, the young fellows of Manhattan Island, customs, instincts, slang, Wisconsin, Georgia, the noble Southern heart, the hot blood, the spirit that will be nothing less than master, the filibuster spirit, the Western man, native-born perceptions, the eye for forms, the perfect models of made things, the wild smack of freedom, California, money, electric-telegraphs, free-trade, iron and the iron mines—recognize without demur those splendid resistless black poems, the steam-ships of the sea-board states, and those other resistless splendid poems, the locomotives, followed through the interior states by trains of rail-road cars.

A word remains to be said, as of one ever present, not yet permitted to be acknowledged, discarded or made dumb by literature, and the results apparent. To the lack of an avowed, empowered, unabashed development of sex, (the only salvation for the same,) and to the fact of speakers and writers fraudulently assuming as always dead what every one knows to be always alive, is attributable the remarkable non-personality and indistinctness of modern productions in books, art, talk; also that in the scanned lives of men and women most of them appear to have béen for some time past of the neuter gender; and also the stinging fact that in orthodox society today. if the dresses were changed, the men might easily pass for women and the women for men.

Infidelism usurps most with fœtid polite face; among the rest infidelism about sex. By silence or obedience the pens of savans, poets, historians, biographers, and the rest, have long connived at the filthy law, and books enslaved to it, that what makes the manhood of a man, that sex, womanhood, maternity, desires, lusty animations, organs, acts, are unmentionable and to be ashamed of, to be driven to skulk out of literature with whatever belongs to them. This filthy law has to be repealed—it stands in the way of great reforms. Of women just as much as men, it is the interest that there should not be infidelism about sex, but perfect faith. Women in These States approach the day of that organic equality with men, without which, I see, men cannot have organic equality among themselves. This empty dish, gallantry, will then be filled with something. This tepid wash, this diluted deferential love, as in songs, fictions, and so forth, is enough to make a man vomit; as to manly friendship, everywhere observed in The States, there is not the first breath of it to be observed in print. I say that the body of a man or woman, the main matter, is so far quite unexpressed in poems; but that the body is to be expressed, and sex is. Of bards for These States, if it come to a question, it is whether they shall celebrate in poems the eternal decency of the amativeness of Nature, the motherhood of all, or whether they shall be the bards of the fashionable delusion of the inherent nastiness of sex, and of the feeble and querulous modesty of deprivation. This is important in poems, because the whole of the other expressions of a nation are but flanges out of its great poems. To me, henceforth, that theory of any thing, no matter what, stagnates in its vitals, cowardly and rotten, while it cannot publicly accept, and publicly name, with specific words, the things on which all existence, all souls, all realization, all decency, all health, all that is worth being here for, all of woman and of man, all beauty, all purity, all sweetness, all friendship, all strength, all life, all immortality depend. The courageous soul, for a year or two to come, may be proved by faith in sex, and by disdaining concessions.

To poets and literats—to every woman and man, today or any day, the conditions of the present, needs, dangers, prejudices, and the like, are the perfect conditions on which we are here, and the conditions for wording the future with undissuadable words. These States, receivers of the stamina of past ages and lands, initiate the outlines of repayment a thousand fold. They fetch the American great masters, waited for by old worlds and new, who accept evil as well as good, ignorance as well as erudition, black as soon as white, foreign-born materials as well as home-born, reject none, force discrepancies into range, surround the whole, concentrate them on present periods and places, show the application to each and any one's body and soul, and show the true use of precedents. Always America will be agitated and turbulent. This day it is taking shape, not to be less so, but to be more so, stormily, capriciously, on native principles, with such vast proportions of parts! As for me, I love screaming, wrestling, boiling-hot days.

Of course, we shall have a national character, an identity. As it ought to be, and as soon as it ought to be, it will be. That, with much else, takes care of itself, is a result, and the cause of greater results. With Ohio,

Illinois, Missouri, Oregon—with the states around the Mexican sea—with cheerfully welcomed immigrants from Europe, Asia, Africa—with Connecticut, Vermont, New Hampshire, Rhode Island—with all varied interests, facts, beliefs, parties, genesis—there is being fused a determined character, fit for the broadest use for the freewomen and freemen of The States, accomplished and to be accomplished, without any exception whatever—each indeed free, each idiomatic, as becomes live states and men, but each adhering to one enclosing general form of politics, manners, talk, personal style, as the plenteous varieties of the race adhere to one physical form. Such character is the brain and spine to all, including literature, including poems. Such character, strong, limber, just, open-mouthed, American-blooded, full of pride, full of ease, of passionate friendliness, is to stand compact upon that vast basis of the supremacy of Individuality— that new moral American continent without which, I see, the physical continent remained incomplete, may-be a carcass, a bloat—that newer America, answering face to face with The States, with ever-satisfying and ever-unsurveyable seas and shores.

Those shores you found. I say you have led The States there—have led Me there. I say that none has ever done, or ever can do, a greater deed for The States, than your deed. Others may line out the lines, build cities, work mines, break up farms; it is yours to have been the original true Captain who put to sea, intuitive, positive, rendering the first report, to be told less by any report, and more by the mariners of a thousand bays, in each tack of their arriving and departing, many years after you.

Receive, dear Master, these statements and assurances through me, for all the young men, and for an earnest that we know none before you, but the best following you; and that we demand to take your name into our keeping, and that we understand what you have indicated, and find the same indicated in ourselves, and that we will stick to it and enlarge upon it through These States.

From *Democratic Vistas*

Political democracy, as it exists and practically works in America, with all its threatening evils, supplies a training-school for making first-class men. It is life's gymnasium, not of good only, but of all. We try often, though we fall back often. A brave delight, fit for freedom's athletes, fills these arenas, and fully satisfies, out of the action in them, irrespective of success. Whatever we do not attain, we at any rate attain the experiences of the fight, the hardening of the strong campaign, and throb with currents of attempt at least. Time is ample. Let the victors come after us. Not for nothing does evil play its part among us. Judging from the main portions of the history of the world, so far, justice is always in jeopardy, peace walks amid hourly pitfalls, and of slavery, misery, meanness, the craft of tyrants and the credulity of the populace, in some of the protean forms, no voice can at any time say, They are not. The clouds break a little, and the sun shines out—but soon and certain the lowering darkness falls again, as if to last forever. Yet is there an immortal courage and prophecy in every sane soul that cannot, must not, under any circumstances, capitulate. *Vive,* the attack—the perennial assault! *Vive,* the unpopular cause—the spirit that audaciously aims—the never-abandoned efforts, pursued the same amid opposing proofs and precedents.

Once, before the war, (Alas! I dare not say how many times the mood has come!) I, too, was fill'd with doubt and gloom. A foreigner, an acute and good man, had impressively said to me, that day—putting in form, indeed, my own observations: "I have travel'd much in the United States, and watched their politicians, and listen'd to the speeches of the candidates, and read the journals, and gone into the public houses, and heard the unguarded talk of men. And I have found your vaunted America honeycomb'd from top to toe with infidelism, even to itself and its own programme. I have mark'd the brazen hell-faces of secession and slavery gazing defiantly from all the windows and doorways. I have everywhere found, primarily, thieves and scalliwags arranging the nominations to offices, and sometimes filling the offices themselves. I have found the north just as full of bad stuff as the south. Of the holders of public office in the Nation or the States or their municipalities, I have found that not one in a hundred has been chosen by any spontaneous selection of the outsiders, the people, but all have been nominated and put through by little or large caucuses of the politicians, and have got in by corrupt rings and electioneering, not capacity or desert. I have noticed how the millions of sturdy farmers and mechanics are thus the helpless supple-jacks of comparatively few politicians. And I have noticed, more and more, the alarming spectacle of parties usurping the government, and openly and shamelessly wielding it for party purposes."

Sad, serious, deep truths. Yet are there other, still deeper, amply confronting, dominating truths. Over those politicians and great and little rings, and over all their insolence and wiles and over the powerfulest parties, looms a power, too sluggish maybe, but ever holding decisions and decrees in hand, ready, with stern process, to execute them as soon as plainly needed—and at times, indeed, summarily crushing to atoms the mightiest parties, even in the hour of their pride.

In saner hours far different are the amounts of these things from what, at first sight, they appear. Though it is no doubt important who is elected governor, mayor, or legislator (and full of dismay when incompetent or vile ones get elected, as they sometimes do,) there are other, quieter contingencies, infinitely more important. Shams, etc., will always be the show, like ocean's scum; enough, if waters deep and clear make up the rest. Enough, that while the piled embroider'd shoddy gaud and fraud spreads to the superficial eye, the hidden warp and weft are genuine, and will wear forever. Enough, in short, that the race, the land which could raise such as the late rebellion, could also put it down.

The average man of a land at last only is important. He, in these States, remains immortal owner and boss, deriving good uses, somehow, out of any sort of servant in office, even the basest; (certain universal requisites, and their settled regularity and protection, being first secured,) a nation like ours, in a sort of geological formation state, trying continually new experiments, choosing new delegations, is not served by the best men only, but sometimes more by those that provoke it—by the combats they arouse. Thus national rage, fury, discussion, etc., better than content. Thus, also, the warning signals, invaluable for after times.

What is more dramatic than the spectacle we have seen repeated, and doubtless long shall see—the popular judgment taking the successful candidates on trial in the offices—standing off, as it were, and observing them and their doings for a while, and always giving, finally, the fit, exactly due reward? I think, after all, the sublimest part of political history, and its culmination, is currently issuing from the American people. I know nothing grander, better exercise, better digestion, more positive proof of the past, the triumphant result of faith in human kind, than a well-contested American national election.

Then still the thought returns, (like the thread-passage in overtures,) giving the key and echo to these pages. When I pass to and fro, different latitudes, different seasons, beholding the crowds of the great cities, New York, Boston, Philadelphia, Cincinnati, Chicago, St. Louis, San Francisco, New Orleans, Baltimore—when I mix with these interminable swarms of alert, turbulent, good-natured, independent citizens, mechanics, clerks, young persons—at the idea of this mass of men, so fresh and free, so loving and so proud, a singular awe falls upon me. I feel, with dejection and amazement, that among our geniuses and talented writers or speakers, few or none have yet really spoken to this people, created a single image-making work for them, or absorb'd the central spirit and the idiosyncrasies which are theirs—and which, thus, in highest ranges, so far remain entirely uncelebrated, unexpress'd.

Dominion strong is the body's; dominion stronger is the mind's. What has fill'd, and fills to-day our intellect, our fancy, furnishing the standards therein, is yet foreign. The great poems, Shakspere included, are poisonous to the idea of the pride and dignity of the common people, the life-blood of democracy. The models of our literature, as we get it from other lands, ultramarine, have had their birth in courts, and bask'd and grown in a castle sunshine; all smells of princes' favors. Of workers of a certain sort, we have, indeed, plenty, contributing after their kind; many elegant, many learn'd, all complacent. But touch'd by the national test, or tried by the standards of democratic personality, they wither to ashes. I say I have not seen a single writer, artist, lecturer, or what not, that has confronted the voiceless but ever erect and active, pervading, underlying will and typic aspiration of the land, in a spirit kindred to itself. Do you call those genteel little creatures American poets? Do you term that perpetual, pistareen, paste-pot work, American art, American drama, taste, verse? I think I hear, echoed as from some mountain-top afar in the west, the scornful laugh of the Genius of these States.

Democracy, in silence, biding its time, ponders its own ideals, not of literature and art only—not of men only, but of women. The idea of the women of America, (extricated from this daze, this fossil and unhealthy air which hangs about the word *lady,*) develop'd, raised to become the robust equals, workers, and, it may be, even practical and political deciders with the men—greater than man, we may admit, through their divine maternity, always their towering, emblematical attribute—but great, at any rate, as man, in all departments; or, rather, capable of being so, soon as they realize it, and can bring themselves to give up toys and fictions, and launch forth, as men do, amid real, independent, stormy life.

Then, as toward our thought's finalè, (and, in that, over-arching the true scholar's lesson,) we have to say there can be no complete or epical presentation of democracy in the aggregate, or anything like it, at this day, because its doctrines will only be effectually incarnated in any one branch, when, in all, their spirit is at the root and centre. Far, far, indeed, stretch, in distance, our Vistas! How much is still to be disentangled, freed! How long it takes to make this American world see that it is, in itself, the final authority and reliance.

Did you, too, O friend, suppose democracy was only for elections, for politics, and for a party name? I say democracy is only of use there that it may pass on and come to its flower and fruits in manners, in the highest forms of interaction between men, and their beliefs—in religion, literature, colleges, and schools—democracy in all public and private life, and in the army and navy. I have intimated that, as a paramount scheme, it has yet few or no full realizers and believers. I do not see, either, that it owes any serious thanks to noted propagandists or champions, or has been essentially help'd, though often harm'd, by them. It has been and is carried on by all the moral forces, and by trade, finance, machinery, intercommunications, and, in fact, by all the developments of history, and can no more be stopp'd than the tides, or the earth in its orbit. Doubtless, also, it resides, crude and latent, well down in the hearts of the fair average of the American-born people, mainly in the agricultural regions. But it is not yet, there or anywhere, the fully-receiv'd, the fervid, the absolute faith.

I submit, therefore, that the fruition of democracy, on aught like a grand scale, resides altogether in the future. As, under any profound and comprehensive view of the gorgeous-composite feudal world, we see in it, through the long ages and cycles of ages, the results of a deep, integral, human and divine principle, or fountain, from which issued laws, ecclesia, manners, institutes, costumes, personalities, poems, (hitherto unequal'd,) faithfully partaking of their source, and indeed only arising either to betoken it, or to furnish parts of that varied-flowing display, whose centre was one and absolute—so, long ages hence, shall the due historian or critic make at least an equal retrospect, an equal history for the democratic principle. It too must be adorn'd, credited with its results—then, when it, with imperial power, through amplest time, has dominated mankind—has been the source and test of all the moral, esthetic, social, political, and religious expressions and institutes of the civilized world—has begotten them in spirit and in form, and has carried them to its own unprecedented heights—has had, (it is possible,) monastics and ascetics, more numerous, more devout than the monks and priests of all previous creeds—has sway'd the ages with a breadth and rectitude tallying Nature's own—has fashion'd, systematized, and triumphantly finish'd and carried out, in its own interest, and with unparallel'd success, a new earth and a new man.

Thus we presume to write, as it were, upon things that exist not, and travel by maps yet unmade, and a blank. But the throes of birth are upon us; and we have something of this advantage in seasons of strong formations, doubts, suspense—for then the afflatus of such themes haply may fall upon us, more or less; and then, hot from surrounding war and revolution, our speech, though without polish'd coherence, and a failure by the standard called criticism, comes forth, real at least as the lightnings.

Notes

1. Walt Whitman, "A Backward Glance O'er Travel'd Roads," in *Leaves of Grass* (Philadelphia: David McKay, 1888), 432–33.
2. Harold Bloom, ed., *Walt Whitman: Selected Poems (American Poets Project)* (New York: Library of America, 2003), xvi–xvii.

Index of Poems *(by title)*

Index of First Lines

Other Books in
The Mystic Poets Series

HAFIZ

Preface by
Ibrahim Gamard,
member of the Sufi Mevlevi Order;
annotator/translator of *Rumi and Islam:
Selections from His Stories, Poems, and
Discourses—Annotated & Explained*

TAGORE

Preface by
Swami Adiswarananda,
Minister and Spiritual Leader of the
Ramakrishna–Vivekananda Center of
New York; author of *Meditation & Its
Practices*

HOPKINS

Preface by
Thomas Ryan, CSP,
author of *Prayer of Heart and Body*

Forthcoming in the Series

HILDEGARD

About SKYLIGHT PATHS Publishing

SkyLight Paths Publishing is creating a place where people of different spiritual traditions come together for challenge and inspiration, a place where we can help each other understand the mystery that lies at the heart of our existence.

Through spirituality, our religious beliefs are increasingly becoming a part of our lives—rather than *apart* from our lives. While many of us may be more interested than ever in spiritual growth, we may be less firmly planted in traditional religion. Yet, we do want to deepen our relationship to the sacred, to learn from our own as well as from other faith traditions, and to practice in new ways.

SkyLight Paths sees both believers and seekers as a community that increasingly transcends traditional boundaries of religion and denomination—people wanting to learn from each other, *walking together, finding the way*.

We at SkyLight Paths take great care to produce beautiful books that present meaningful spiritual content in a form that reflects the art of making high quality books. Therefore, we want to acknowledge those who contributed to the production of this book.

PRODUCTION
Bernadine Dawes & Tim Holtz

EDITORIAL
Sarah McBride, Maura D. Shaw
& Emily Wichland

JACKET DESIGN
Bridgett Taylor & Jenny Buono

TEXT DESIGN
Bridgett Taylor

PRINTING & BINDING
Friesens Corporation, Manitoba, Canada

Other Interesting Books—Spirituality

Lighting the Lamp of Wisdom: *A Week Inside a Yoga Ashram*
by *John Ittner*; Foreword by *Dr. David Frawley*

This insider's guide to Hindu spiritual life takes you into a typical week of retreat inside a yoga ashram to demystify the experience and show you what to expect from your own visit. Includes a discussion of worship services, meditation and yoga classes, chanting and music, work practice, and more.

6 x 9, 192 pp, b/w photographs, Quality PB, ISBN 1-893361-52-7 **$15.95;**
HC, ISBN 1-893361-37-3 **$24.95**

Waking Up: *A Week Inside a Zen Monastery*
by *Jack Maguire*; Foreword by *John Daido Loori, Roshi*

An essential guide to what it's like to spend a week inside a Zen Buddhist monastery.

6 x 9, 224 pp, b/w photographs, Quality PB, ISBN 1-893361-55-1 **$16.95;**
HC, ISBN 1-893361-13-6 **$21.95**

Making a Heart for God: *A Week Inside a Catholic Monastery*
by *Dianne Aprile*; Foreword by *Brother Patrick Hart, ocso*

This essential guide to experiencing life in a Catholic monastery takes you to the Abbey of Gethsemani—the Trappist monastery in Kentucky that was home to author Thomas Merton—to explore the details. "More balanced and informative than the popular *The Cloister Walk* by Kathleen Norris." —*Choice: Current Reviews for Academic Libraries*

6 x 9, 224 pp, b/w photographs, Quality PB, ISBN 1-893361-49-7 **$16.95;**
HC, ISBN 1-893361-14-4 **$21.95**

Come and Sit: *A Week Inside Meditation Centers*
by *Marcia Z. Nelson*; Foreword by *Wayne Teasdale*

The insider's guide to meditation in a variety of different spiritual traditions. Traveling through Buddhist, Hindu, Christian, Jewish, and Sufi traditions, this essential guide takes you to different meditation centers to meet the teachers and students and learn about the practices, demystifying the meditation experience.

6 x 9, 224 pp, b/w photographs, Quality PB, ISBN 1-893361-35-7 **$16.95**

Or phone, fax, mail or e-mail to: SKYLIGHT PATHS Publishing
Sunset Farm Offices, Route 4 • P.O. Box 237 • Woodstock, Vermont 05091
Tel: (802) 457-4000 • Fax: (802) 457-4004 • www.skylightpaths.com
Credit card orders: (800) 962-4544 (8:30AM–5:30PM ET Monday–Friday)
Generous discounts on quantity orders. SATISFACTION GUARANTEED. Prices subject to change.

Spiritual Biography

The Life of Evelyn Underhill
An Intimate Portrait of the Groundbreaking Author of Mysticism
by *Margaret Cropper;* Foreword by *Dana Greene*

Evelyn Underhill was a passionate writer and teacher who wrote elegantly on mysticism, worship, and devotional life. This is the story of how she made her way toward spiritual maturity, from her early days of agnosticism to the years when her influence was felt throughout the world.

6 x 9, 288 pp, 5 b/w photos, Quality PB, ISBN 1-893361-70-5 **$18.95**

Zen Effects: *The Life of Alan Watts*
by *Monica Furlong*

The first and only full-length biography of one of the most charismatic spiritual leaders of the twentieth century—now back in print!

Through his widely popular books and lectures, Alan Watts (1915–1973) did more to introduce Eastern philosophy and religion to Western minds than any figure before or since. Here is the only biography of this charismatic figure, who served as Zen teacher, Anglican priest, lecturer, academic, entertainer, a leader of the San Francisco renaissance, and author of more than 30 books, including *The Way of Zen, Psychotherapy East and West* and *The Spirit of Zen.*

6 x 9, 264 pp, Quality PB, ISBN 1-893361-32-2 **$16.95**

Simone Weil: *A Modern Pilgrimage*
by *Robert Coles*

The extraordinary life of the spiritual philosopher who's been called both saint and madwoman.

The French writer and philosopher Simone Weil (1906–1943) devoted her life to a search for God—while avoiding membership in organized religion. Robert Coles' intriguing study of Weil details her short, eventful life, and is an insightful portrait of the beloved and controversial thinker whose life and writings influenced many (from T. S. Eliot to Adrienne Rich to Albert Camus), and continue to inspire seekers everywhere.

6 x 9, 208 pp, Quality PB, ISBN 1-893361-34-9 **$16.95**

Mahatma Gandhi: *His Life and Ideas*
by *Charles F. Andrews;* Foreword by *Dr. Arun Gandhi*

An intimate biography of one of the greatest social and religious reformers of the modern world.

Examines from a contemporary Christian activist's point of view the religious ideas and political dynamics that influenced the birth of the peaceful resistance movement, the primary tool that Gandhi and the people of his homeland would use to gain India its freedom from British rule. An ideal introduction to the life and life's work of this great spiritual leader.

6 x 9, 336 pp, 5 b/w photos, Quality PB, ISBN 1-893361-89-6 **$18.95**

Spiritual Practice

The Sacred Art of Bowing: *Preparing to Practice*
by *Andi Young*

This informative and inspiring introduction to bowing—and related spiritual practices—shows you how to do it, why it's done, and what spiritual benefits it has to offer. Incorporates interviews, personal stories, illustrations of bowing in practice, advice on how you can incorporate bowing into your daily life, and how bowing can deepen spiritual understanding.

5½ x 8½, 128 pp, b/w illus., Quality PB, ISBN 1-893361-82-9 **$14.95**

Praying with Our Hands: *Twenty-One Practices of Embodied Prayer from the World's Spiritual Traditions*
by *Jon M. Sweeney;* Photographs by *Jennifer J. Wilson;*
Foreword by *Mother Tessa Bielecki;* Afterword by *Taitetsu Unno, PhD*

A spiritual guidebook for bringing prayer into our bodies.

This inspiring book of reflections and accompanying photographs shows us twenty-one simple ways of using our hands to speak to God, to enrich our devotion and ritual. All express the various approaches of the world's religious traditions to bringing the body into worship. Spiritual traditions represented include Anglican, Sufi, Zen, Roman Catholic, Yoga, Shaker, Hindu, Jewish, Pentecostal, Eastern Orthodox, and many others.

8 x 8, 96 pp, 22 duotone photographs, Quality PB, ISBN 1-893361-16-0 **$16.95**

The Sacred Art of Listening
Forty Reflections for Cultivating a Spiritual Practice
by *Kay Lindahl;* Illustrations by *Amy Schnapper*

More than ever before, we need to embrace the skills and practice of listening. You will learn to: Speak clearly from your heart • Communicate with courage • Heighten your awareness for deep listening • Enhance your ability to listen to people with different belief systems.

8 x 8, 160 pp, Illus., Quality PB, ISBN 1-893361-44-6 **$16.99**

Labyrinths from the Outside In
Walking to Spiritual Insight—A Beginner's Guide
by *Donna Schaper* and *Carole Ann Camp*

The user-friendly, interfaith guide to making and using labyrinths— for meditation, prayer, and celebration.

Labyrinth walking is a spiritual exercise anyone can do. This accessible guide unlocks the mysteries of the labyrinth for all of us, providing ideas for using the labyrinth walk for prayer, meditation, and celebrations to mark the most important moments in life. Includes instructions for making a labyrinth of your own and finding one in your area.

6 x 9, 208 pp, b/w illus. and photographs, Quality PB, ISBN 1-893361-18-7 **$16.95**

SkyLight Illuminations Series
Andrew Harvey, series editor

Offers today's spiritual seeker an enjoyable entry into the great classic texts of the world's spiritual traditions. Each classic is presented in an accessible translation, with facing pages of guided commentary from experts, giving you the keys you need to understand the history, context, and meaning of the text. This series enables readers of all backgrounds to experience and understand classic spiritual texts directly, and to make them a part of their lives. Andrew Harvey writes the foreword to each volume, an insightful, personal introduction to each classic.

Bhagavad Gita: *Annotated & Explained*
Translation by *Shri Purohit Swami;* Annotation by *Kendra Crossen Burroughs*

"The very best Gita for first-time readers." —Ken Wilber

Millions of people turn daily to India's most beloved holy book, whose universal appeal has made it popular with non-Hindus and Hindus alike. This edition introduces you to the characters, explains references and philosophical terms, shares the interpretations of famous spiritual leaders and scholars, and more.
5¹⁄₂ x 8¹⁄₂, 192 pp, Quality PB, ISBN 1-893361-28-4 **$16.95**

The Way of a Pilgrim: *Annotated & Explained*
Translation and annotation by *Gleb Pokrovsky*

This classic of Russian spirituality is the delightful account of one man who sets out to learn the prayer of the heart—also known as the "Jesus prayer"—and how the practice transforms his life.
5¹⁄₂ x 8¹⁄₂, 160 pp, Illus., Quality PB, ISBN 1-893361-31-4 **$14.95**

The Gospel of Thomas: *Annotated & Explained*
Translation and annotation by *Stevan Davies*

Discovered in 1945, this collection of aphoristic sayings sheds new light on the origins of Christianity and the intriguing figure of Jesus, portraying the Kingdom of God as a present fact about the world, rather than a future promise or future threat. This edition guides you through the text with annotations that focus on the meaning of the sayings.
5¹⁄₂ x 8¹⁄₂, 192 pp, Quality PB, ISBN 1-893361-45-4 **$16.95**

Rumi and Islam: *Selections from His Stories, Poems, and Discourses—Annotated & Explained*
Translation and annotation by *Ibrahim Gamard*

Offers a new way of thinking about Rumi's poetry. Ibrahim Gamard focuses on Rumi's place within the Sufi tradition of Islam, providing you with insight into the mystical side of the religion—one that has love of God at its core and sublime wisdom teachings as its pathways.
5¹⁄₂ x 8¹⁄₂, 240 pp, Quality PB, ISBN 1-59473-002-4 **$15.99**

SkyLight Illuminations Series
Andrew Harvey, series editor

Zohar: *Annotated & Explained*
Translation and annotation by *Daniel C. Matt*

The cornerstone text of Kabbalah.

Guides you step by step through the midrash, mystical fantasy, and Hebrew scripture that make up the *Zohar*, explaining the inner meanings in facing-page commentary. Ideal for readers without any prior knowledge of Jewish mysticism.

5½ x 8½, 176 pp, Quality PB, ISBN 1-893361-51-9 **$15.99**

Selections from the Gospel of Sri Ramakrishna
Annotated & Explained
Translation by *Swami Nikhilananda*; Annotation by *Kendra Crossen Burroughs*

Introduces the fascinating world of the Indian mystic and the universal appeal of his message that has inspired millions of devotees for more than a century. Selections from the original text and insightful yet unobtrusive commentary highlight the most important and inspirational teachings. Ideal for readers without any prior knowledge of Hinduism.

5½ x 8½, 240 pp, b/w photographs, Quality PB, ISBN 1-893361-46-2 **$16.95**

Dhammapada: *Annotated & Explained*
Translation by *Max Müller* and revised by *Jack Maguire;*
Annotation by *Jack Maguire*

The classic of Buddhist spiritual practice.

The Dhammapada—words spoken by the Buddha himself over 2,500 years ago—is notoriously difficult to understand for the first-time reader. Now you can experience it with understanding even if you have no previous knowledge of Buddhism. Enlightening facing-page commentary explains all the names, terms, and references, giving you deeper insight into the text.

5½ x 8½, 160 pp, b/w photographs, Quality PB, ISBN 1-893361-42-X **$14.95**

Hasidic Tales: *Annotated & Explained*
Translation and annotation by *Rabbi Rami Shapiro*

The legendary tales of the impassioned Hasidic rabbis.

The allegorical quality of Hasidic tales can be perplexing. Here, they are presented as stories rather than parables, making them accessible and meaningful. Each demonstrates the spiritual power of unabashed joy, offers lessons for leading a holy life, and reminds us that the Divine can be found in the everyday. Annotations explain theological concepts, introduce major characters, and clarify references unfamiliar to most readers.

5½ x 8½, 240 pp, Quality PB, ISBN 1-893361-86-1 **$16.95**

Meditation/Prayer

Finding Grace at the Center: *The Beginning of Centering Prayer*
by *M. Basil Pennington, ocso, Thomas Keating, ocso,* and *Thomas E. Clarke, sj*

The book that helped launch the *Centering Prayer* "movement." Explains the prayer of *The Cloud of Unknowing,* posture and relaxation, the three simple rules of centering prayer, and how to cultivate centering prayer throughout all aspects of your life.

5 x 7¼,112 pp, HC, ISBN 1-893361-69-1 **$14.95**

Prayers to an Evolutionary God
by *William Cleary;* Afterword by *Diarmuid O'Murchu*

How is it possible to pray when God is dislocated from heaven, dispersed all around us, and more of a creative force than an all-knowing father? In this unique collection of eighty prose prayers and related commentary, William Cleary considers new ways of thinking about God and the world around us. Inspired by the spiritual and scientific teachings of Diarmuid O'Murchu and Teilhard de Chardin, Cleary reveals that religion and science can be combined to create an expanding view of the universe—an evolutionary faith.

6 x 9, 208 pp, HC, ISBN 1-59473-006-7 **$21.99**

Meditation without Gurus
A Guide to the Heart of Practice
by *Clark Strand*

Short, compelling reflections show you how to make meditation a part of your daily life, without the complication of gurus, mantras, retreats, or treks to distant mountains. This enlightening book strips the practice down to its essential heart—simplicity, lightness, and peace—showing you that the most important part of practice is not whether you can get in the full lotus position, but rather your ability to become fully present in the moment.

5½ x 8½, 192 pp, Quality PB, ISBN 1-893361-93-4 **$16.95**

Meditation & Its Practices
A Definitive Guide to Techniques and Traditions of Meditation in Yoga and Vedanta
by *Swami Adiswarananda*

The complete sourcebook for exploring Hinduism's two most time-honored traditions of meditation.

Drawing on both classic and contemporary sources, this comprehensive sourcebook outlines the scientific, psychological, and spiritual elements of Yoga and Vedanta meditation.

6 x 9, 504 pp, HC, ISBN 1-893361-83-7 **$34.95**

Nature Essay

Autumn: *A Spiritual Biography of the Season*
Edited by *Gary Schmidt* and *Susan M. Felch*; Illustrations by *Mary Azarian*

Discover how this transitional season reveals both the abundance and the limitations of our everyday lives.

Autumn is a season of fruition and harvest, of thanksgiving and celebration of abundance and goodness of the earth. But it is also a season that starkly and realistically encourages us to see the limitations of our time.

Warm and poignant pieces by Wendell Berry, David James Duncan, Robert Frost, A. Bartlett Giamatti, Kimiko Hahn, P. D. James, Julian of Norwich, Garret Keizer, Tracy Kidder, Anne Lamott, May Sarton, and many others in this beautiful book rejoice in autumn as a time of preparation and reflection, when the results of hard labor are ripe for harvest.

6 x 9, 320 pp, 5 b/w illus., HC, ISBN 1-59473-005-9 **$22.99**

Winter: *A Spiritual Biography of the Season*
Edited by *Gary Schmidt* and *Susan M. Felch*; Illustrations by *Barry Moser*

Explore how the dormancy of winter can be a time of spiritual preparation and transformation.

In thirty stirring pieces, *Winter* delves into the varied feelings that winter conjures in us, calling up both the barrenness and the beauty of the natural world in wintertime. Includes selections by Will Campbell, Rachel Carson, Annie Dillard, Donald Hall, Ron Hansen, Jane Kenyon, Jamaica Kincaid, Barry Lopez, Kathleen Norris, John Updike, E. B. White, and many others.

"This outstanding anthology features top-flight nature and spirituality writers on the fierce, inexorable season of winter.... Remarkably lively and warm, despite the icy subject."—★*Publishers Weekly* Starred Review

6 x 9, 288 pp, 6 b/w illus., Deluxe PB w/flaps, ISBN 1-893361-92-6 **$18.95**
HC, ISBN 1-893361-53-5 **$21.95**

Children's Spiritual Biography

Ten Amazing People
And How They Changed the World
by *Maura D. Shaw*; Foreword by *Dr. Robert Coles*
Full-color illus. by *Stephen Marchesi*

For ages 7 & up

> Black Elk • Dorothy Day • Malcolm X • Mahatma Gandhi •
> Martin Luther King, Jr. • Mother Teresa • Janusz Korczak •
> Desmond Tutu • Thich Nhat Hanh • Albert Schweitzer

This vivid, inspirational, and authoritative book will open new possibilities for children by telling the stories of how ten of the past century's greatest leaders changed the world in important ways.

8½ x 11, 48 pp, HC, Full-color illus., ISBN 1-893361-47-0 **$17.95**

A new series: Spiritual Biographies for Young People

Thich Nhat Hanh: *Buddhism in Action*
by *Maura D. Shaw*; Full-color illus. by *Stephen Marchesi*

For ages 7 & up

Warm illustrations, photos, age-appropriate activities, and Thich Nhat Hanh's own poems introduce a great man to children in a way they can understand and enjoy. Includes a list of important Buddhist words to know.

6¾ x 8¾, 32 pp, HC, Full-color illus., ISBN 1-893361-87-X **$12.95**

Gandhi: *India's Great Soul*
by *Maura D. Shaw*; Full-color illus. by *Stephen Marchesi*

For ages 7 & up

There are a number of biographies of Gandhi written for young readers, but this is the only one that balances a simple text with illustrations, photographs, and activities that encourage children and adults to talk about how to make changes happen without violence. Introduces children to important concepts of freedom, equality, and justice among people of all backgrounds and religions.

6¾ x 8¾, 32 pp, HC, Full-color illus., ISBN 1-893361-91-8 **$12.95**

Dorothy Day: *A Catholic Life of Action*
by *Maura D. Shaw*; Full-color illus. by *Stephen Marchesi*

For ages 7 & up

Introduces children to one of the most inspiring women of the twentieth century, a down-to-earth spiritual leader who saw the presence of God in every person she met. Includes practical activities, a timeline, and a list of important words to know.

6¾ x 8¾, 32 pp, HC, Full-color illus., ISBN 1-59473-011-3 **$12.99**

Children's Spirituality

Where Does God Live?

For ages 3–6

by *August Gold* and *Matthew J. Perlman*

Using simple, everyday examples that children can relate to, this colorful book helps young readers develop a personal understanding of God.

10 x 8½, 32 pp, Quality PB, Full-color photo illus., ISBN 1-893361-39-X **$8.99**

God in Between

For ages 4 & up

by *Sandy Eisenberg Sasso*; Full-color illus. by *Sally Sweetland*

If you wanted to find God, where would you look? A magical, mythical tale that teaches that God can be found where we are: within all of us and the relationships between us. "This happy and wondrous book takes our children on a sweet and holy journey into God's presence." —Rabbi Wayne Dosick, PhD, author of *The Business Bible* and *Soul Judaism*

9 x 12, 32 pp, HC, Full-color illus., ISBN 1-879045-86-9 **$16.95**

Cain & Abel: *Finding the Fruits of Peace*

For ages 5 & up

by *Sandy Eisenberg Sasso*; Full-color illus. by *Joani Keller Rothenberg*

A sensitive recasting of the ancient tale shows we have the power to deal with anger in positive ways. Provides questions for kids and adults to explore together. "Editor's Choice"—American Library Association's *Booklist*

9 x 12, 32 pp, HC, Full-color illus., ISBN 1-58023-123-3 **$16.95**

In Our Image: *God's First Creatures*

For ages 4 & up

by *Nancy Sohn Swartz*; Full-color illus. by *Melanie Hall*

A playful new twist on the Creation story—from the perspective of the animals. Celebrates the interconnectedness of nature and the harmony of all living things.

"The vibrantly colored illustrations nearly leap off the page in this delightful interpretation." —*School Library Journal*

"A message all children should hear, presented in words and pictures that children will find irresistible." —Rabbi Harold Kushner, author of *When Bad Things Happen to Good People*

9 x 12, 32 pp, HC, Full-color illus., ISBN 1-879045-99-0 **$16.95**

Children's Spirituality

Because Nothing Looks Like God

For ages 4 & up

by *Lawrence and Karen Kushner*
Full-color illus. by *Dawn W. Majewski*

MULTICULTURAL, NONDENOMINATIONAL, NONSECTARIAN

Real-life examples of happiness and sadness—from goodnight stories, to the hope and fear felt the first time at bat, to the closing moments of life—introduce children to the possibilities of spiritual life. A vibrant way for children—and their adults—to explore what, where, and how God is in our lives.

11 x 8½, 32 pp, HC, Full-color illus., ISBN 1-58023-092-X **$16.95**
Also available: **Teacher's Guide**, 8½ x 11, 22 pp, PB, ISBN 1-58023-140-3 **$6.95** For ages 5–8

For ages 0–4

Where Is God? (A Board Book)

by *Lawrence and Karen Kushner*; Full-color illus. by *Dawn W. Majewski*

A gentle way for young children to explore how God is with us every day, in every way. Abridged from *Because Nothing Looks Like God* by Lawrence and Karen Kushner and specially adapted to board book format to delight and inspire young readers.

5 x 5, 24 pp, Board, Full-color illus., ISBN 1-893361-17-9 **$7.95**

For ages 0–4

What Does God Look Like? (A Board Book)

by *Lawrence and Karen Kushner*; Full-color illus. by *Dawn W. Majewski*

A simple way for young children to explore the ways that we "see" God. Abridged from *Because Nothing Looks Like God* by Lawrence and Karen Kushner and specially adapted to board book format to delight and inspire young readers.

5 x 5, 24 pp, Board, Full-color illus., ISBN 1-893361-23-3 **$7.95**

For ages 0–4

How Does God Make Things Happen? (A Board Book)

by *Lawrence and Karen Kushner*; Full-color illus. by *Dawn W. Majewski*

A charming invitation for young children to explore how God makes things happen in our world. Abridged from *Because Nothing Looks Like God* by Lawrence and Karen Kushner and specially adapted to board book format to delight and inspire young readers.

5 x 5, 24 pp, Board, Full-color illus., ISBN 1-893361-24-1 **$7.95**

For ages 0–4

What Is God's Name? (A Board Book)

by *Sandy Eisenberg Sasso*; Full-color illus. by *Phoebe Stone*

Everyone and everything in the world has a name. What is God's name? Abridged from the award-winning *In God's Name* by Sandy Eisenberg Sasso and specially adapted to board book format to delight and inspire young readers.

5 x 5, 24 pp, Board, Full-color illus., ISBN 1-893361-10-1 **$7.99**

Spirituality

Journeys of Simplicity: *Traveling Light with Thomas Merton, Bashō, Edward Abbey, Annie Dillard & Others*
by *Philip Harnden*

Offers vignettes of forty "travelers" and the few ordinary things they carried with them—from place to place, from day to day, from birth to death. What Thoreau took to Walden Pond. What Thomas Merton packed for his final trip to Asia. What Annie Dillard keeps in her writing tent. What an impoverished cook served M. F. K. Fisher for dinner. Much more.

"'How much should I carry with me?' is the quintessential question for any journey, especially the journey of life. Herein you'll find sage, sly, wonderfully subversive advice." —Bill McKibben, author of *The End of Nature* and *Enough*

5 x 7¼, 128 pp, HC, ISBN 1-893361-76-4 **$16.95**

What Matters: *Spiritual Nourishment for Head and Heart*
by *Frederick Franck*

Savor what truly matters in your own life.

This elegantly simple book of reflections presents the rich harvest of a lifetime of thinking, feeling, and seeing by an artist whose vital spirituality has inspired hundreds of thousands of readers and students through his art, books, and workshops. The pithy, sometimes humorous, always wise contemplations reveal Franck's lifelong confrontation with the human in himself and others.

5 x 7¼, 144 pp, 50+ b/w illus., HC, ISBN 1-59473-013-X **$16.99**

Spiritually Incorrect: *Finding God in All the Wrong Places*
by *Dan Wakefield;* Illus. by *Marian DelVecchio*

Spirituality is full of rules.
You need to find your own way straight through them.

Award-winning author Dan Wakefield dares to ask the risky (and sometimes hilarious) questions about spirituality. His insightful reflections break down the barriers that lie in the way of spiritual fulfillment, showing you that it's possible—and imperative—for you to discover a rewarding spiritual life that fits your own personality, your own path.

5½ x 8½, 192 pp, b/w illus., HC, ISBN 1-893361-88-8 **$21.95**

Interspirituality

A Walk with Four Spiritual Guides
Krishna, Buddha, Jesus, and Ramakrishna
by *Andrew Harvey*

> Andrew Harvey's warm and personal introduction to each guide
> offers his own experiences of learning from their wisdom.

The core of their most important teachings—along with annotations from expert scholars and introductions from Andrew Harvey, one of the great spiritual thinkers of our time—now are all in one beautiful volume.

5½ x 8½, 192 pp, 10 b/w photos & illus., Hardcover, ISBN 1-893361-73-X **$21.95**

The Alphabet of Paradise: *An A–Z of Spirituality for Everyday Life*
by *Howard Cooper*

> "An extraordinary book." —Karen Armstrong

In twenty-six engaging chapters—from A to Z—Cooper spiritually illuminates the subjects of daily life, using an ancient Jewish mystical method of interpretation that reveals both the literal and more allusive meanings of each. Topics include: Awe, Bodies, Creativity, Dreams, Emotions, Sports, and more.

5 x 7¾, 224 pp, Quality PB, ISBN 1-893361-80-2 **$16.95**

Daughters of the Desert: *Tales of Remarkable Women from Christian, Jewish, and Muslim Traditions*
by *Claire Rudolf Murphy, Meghan Nuttall Sayres, Mary Cronk Farrell, Sarah Conover,* and *Betsy Wharton*

> Breathes new life into the old tales of our female ancestors in faith.

The authors use traditional scriptural passages as their starting points, then with vivid detail fill in historical context and place. Chapters reveal the voices of Sarah, Hagar, Huldah, Esther, Salome, Mary Magdalene, Lydia, Khadija, Fatima, and many more. Historical fiction ideal for readers of all ages.

5½ x 8½, 192 pp, HC, ISBN 1-893361-72-1 **$19.95**

Bede Griffiths: *An Introduction to His Interspiritual Thought*
by *Wayne Teasdale*

> The first in-depth study of Bede Griffiths'
> contemplative experience and thought.

Wayne Teasdale, a longtime personal friend and student of Griffiths, creates in this intimate portrait an intriguing view into the beliefs and life of this champion of interreligious acceptance and harmony. Explains key terms that form the basis of Griffiths' contemplative understanding, and the essential characteristics of his theology as they relate to the Hindu and Christian traditions.

6 x 9, 288 pp, Quality PB, ISBN 1-893361-77-2 **$18.95**

Global Spiritual Perspectives

Spiritual Perspectives on America's Role as Superpower
by *the Editors at SkyLight Paths*

Are we the world's good neighbor or a global bully?

Explores broader issues surrounding the use of American power around the world, including in Iraq and the Middle East. From a spiritual perspective, what are America's responsibilities as the only remaining superpower?

CONTRIBUTORS:

Dr. Beatrice Bruteau • Rev. Dr. Joan Brown Campbell • Tony Campolo • Rev. Forrest Church • Lama Surya Das • Matthew Fox • Kabir Helminski • Thich Nhat Hanh • Eboo Patel • Abbot M. Basil Pennington, ocso • Dennis Prager • Rosemary Radford Ruether • Wayne Teasdale • Rev. William McD. Tully • Rabbi Arthur Waskow • John Wilson

5¹/₂ x 8¹/₂, 256 pp, Quality PB, ISBN 1-893361-81-0 **$16.95**

Spiritual Perspectives on Globalization, 2nd Edition
Making Sense of Economic and Cultural Upheaval
by *Ira Rifkin; Foreword by Dr. David Little, Harvard Divinity School*

What is globalization? What are spiritually minded people saying and doing about it?

This lucid introduction surveys the religious landscape, explaining in clear and nonjudgmental language the beliefs that motivate spiritual leaders, activists, theologians, academics, and others involved on all sides of the issue. This edition includes a new Afterword and Discussion Guide designed for group use.

5¹/₂ x 8¹/₂, 256 pp, Quality PB, ISBN 1-59473-045-8 **$16.99**

Spiritual Innovators: *Seventy-Five Extraordinary People Who Changed the World in the Past Century*
Edited by *Ira Rifkin* and *the Editors at SkyLight Paths;*
Foreword by *Robert Coles*

Black Elk, Bede Griffiths, H. H. the Dalai Lama, Abraham Joshua Heschel, Martin Luther King, Jr., Krishnamurti, C. S. Lewis, Aimee Semple McPherson, Thomas Merton, Simone Weil, and many more.

Profiles of the most important spiritual leaders of the past one hundred years. An invaluable reference of twentieth-century religion and an inspiring resource for spiritual challenge today. Authoritative list of seventy-five includes mystics and martyrs, intellectuals and charismatics from the East and West. For each, includes a brief biography, inspiring quotes, and resources for more in-depth study.

6 x 9, 304 pp, b/w photographs, Quality PB, ISBN 1-893361-50-0 **$16.95;**
HC, ISBN 1-893361-43-8 **$24.95**

Religious Etiquette/Reference

How to Be a Perfect Stranger, 3rd Edition
The Essential Religious Etiquette Handbook
Edited by *Stuart M. Matlins* and *Arthur J. Magida*

**The indispensable guidebook to help the well-meaning guest
when visiting other people's religious ceremonies.**

A straightforward guide to the rituals and celebrations of the major religions
and denominations in the United States and Canada from the perspective of an
interested guest of any other faith, based on information obtained from author-
ities of each religion. Belongs in every living room, library, and office.

COVERS:

African American Methodist Churches • Assemblies of God • Baha'i • Baptist
• Buddhist • Christian Church (Disciples of Christ) • Christian Science (Church
of Christ, Scientist) • Churches of Christ • Episcopalian and Anglican • Hindu
• Islam • Jehovah's Witnesses • Jewish • Lutheran • Mennonite/Amish •
Methodist • Mormon (Church of Jesus Christ of Latter-day Saints) • Native
American/First Nations • Orthodox Churches • Pentecostal Church of God •
Presbyterian • Quaker (Religious Society of Friends) • Reformed Church in
America/Canada • Roman Catholic • Seventh-day Adventist • Sikh • Unitarian
Universalist • United Church of Canada • United Church of Christ

6 x 9, 432 pp, Quality PB, ISBN 1-893361-67-5 **$19.95**

What You Will See Inside a Mosque
by *Aisha Karen Khan*; Photographs by *Aaron Pepis*

**A colorful, fun-to-read introduction that explains the ways
and whys of Muslim faith and worship.**

Visual and informative, featuring full-page pictures and concise descriptions of
what is happening, the objects used, the spiritual leaders and laypeople who
have specific roles, and the spiritual intent of the believers.

Ideal for children as well as teachers, parents, librarians, clergy, and lay leaders
who want to demystify the celebrations and ceremonies of Islam throughout
the year, as well as encourage understanding and tolerance among different
faith traditions.

8¹/₂ x 10¹/₂, 32 pp, Full-color photographs, HC, ISBN 1-893361-60-8 **$16.95**